Achieve great Chemistry with CGP!

Let's deal with the bad news first: the new Grade 9-1 GCSE Chemistry courses are tougher than ever, so you'll need to be at the top of your game on exam day.

Here's the good news: this fantastic CGP book is absolutely jam-packed with all the exam-style practice you'll need — it even covers all the new required practicals.

And since you'll be tested on a wide range of topics in the real exams, we've also included a section of mixed questions to keep you on your toes!

CGP — still the best! ☺

Our sole aim here at CGP is to produce the highest quality books — carefully written, immaculately presented and dangerously close to being funny.

Then we work our socks off to get them out to you — at the cheapest possible prices.

Contents

☑ Use the tick boxes to check off the topics you've completed.

Chapter C5 — Chemical Analysis

Chapter C6 — Making Useful Chemicals

Mixed Questions

Published by CGP

Editors: Emily Forsberg, Emily Howe, Paul Jordin

Contributors: Ian Davis, Alison Dennis, Chris Workman

With thanks to Barrie Crowther and Glenn Rogers for the proofreading.

With thanks to Ana Pungartnik for the copyright research.

ISBN: 978 1 78294 506 2

Data on the graph on page 13 showing the change in atmospheric CO_2 concentration provided by Carbon Cycle and Greenhouse Gases group, 325 Broadway R/CSD, Boulder, CO 80305 (http://esrl.noaa.gov/gmd/ccgg/)

Data on the graph on page 13 showing the change in global temperature from GISTEMP Team, 2015: GISS Surface Temperature Analysis (GISTEMP). NASA Goddard Institute for Space Studies. Dataset accessed 2016-04-11 at http://data.giss.nasa.gov/gistemp/.

Graph on page 13 showing CO_2 emissions for UK and Crown Dependencies contains public sector information licensed under the Open Government Licence v3.0. http://www.nationalarchives.gov.uk/doc/open-government-licence/version/3/

Data to construct graph showing sea level change on page 13 provided by the JPL PODAAC, in support of the NASA's MEaSUREs program.

www.cgpbooks.co.uk
Clipart from Corel®
Printed by Elanders Ltd, Newcastle upon Tyne

Based on the classic CGP style created by Richard Parsons.

How to Use This Book

- Hold the book <u>upright</u>, approximately <u>50 cm</u> from your face, ensuring that the text looks like <u>this</u>, not sᴉɥʇ. Alternatively, place the book on a <u>horizontal</u> surface (e.g. a table or desk) and sit adjacent to the book, at a distance which doesn't make the text too small to read.

- In case of emergency, press the two halves of the book together <u>firmly</u> in order to close.

- Before attempting to use this book, familiarise yourself with the following <u>safety information</u>:

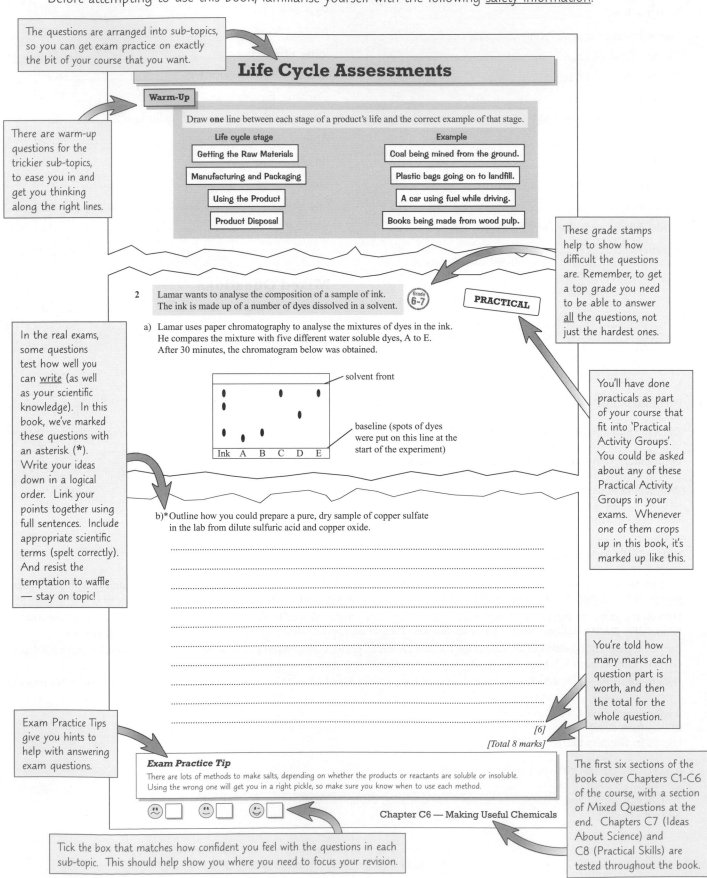

The questions are arranged into sub-topics, so you can get exam practice on exactly the bit of your course that you want.

Life Cycle Assessments

Warm-Up

There are warm-up questions for the trickier sub-topics, to ease you in and get you thinking along the right lines.

Draw **one** line between each stage of a product's life and the correct example of that stage.

Life cycle stage
- Getting the Raw Materials
- Manufacturing and Packaging
- Using the Product
- Product Disposal

Example
- Coal being mined from the ground.
- Plastic bags going on to landfill.
- A car using fuel while driving.
- Books being made from wood pulp.

These grade stamps help to show how difficult the questions are. Remember, to get a top grade you need to be able to answer <u>all</u> the questions, not just the hardest ones.

2   Lamar wants to analyse the composition of a sample of ink. The ink is made up of a number of dyes dissolved in a solvent.   **Grade 6-7**   **PRACTICAL**

In the real exams, some questions test how well you can <u>write</u> (as well as your scientific knowledge). In this book, we've marked these questions with an asterisk (*****). Write your ideas down in a logical order. Link your points together using full sentences. Include appropriate scientific terms (spelt correctly). And resist the temptation to waffle — stay on topic!

a)   Lamar uses paper chromatography to analyse the mixtures of dyes in the ink. He compares the mixture with five different water soluble dyes, A to E. After 30 minutes, the chromatogram below was obtained.

— solvent front

— baseline (spots of dyes were put on this line at the start of the experiment)

Ink A B C D E

You'll have done practicals as part of your course that fit into 'Practical Activity Groups'. You could be asked about any of these Practical Activity Groups in your exams. Whenever one of them crops up in this book, it's marked up like this.

b)* Outline how you could prepare a pure, dry sample of copper sulfate in the lab from dilute sulfuric acid and copper oxide.

....

....

....

....

....

....

....

....

....

....

....

You're told how many marks each question part is worth, and then the total for the whole question.

[6]

[Total 8 marks]

Exam Practice Tips give you hints to help with answering exam questions.

Exam Practice Tip
There are lots of methods to make salts, depending on whether the products or reactants are soluble or insoluble. Using the wrong one will get you in a right pickle, so make sure you know when to use each method.

😌 ☐   🙂 ☐   😊 ☐

Chapter C6 — Making Useful Chemicals

The first six sections of the book cover Chapters C1-C6 of the course, with a section of Mixed Questions at the end. Chapters C7 (Ideas About Science) and C8 (Practical Skills) are tested throughout the book.

Tick the box that matches how confident you feel with the questions in each sub-topic. This should help show you where you need to focus your revision.

States of Matter

Identify which of the following statements is false.
Place a tick (✓) in the box next to the correct answer.

Particles in liquids are free to move past each other but tend to stick together. ☐

Solids have a definite shape and volume. ☐

There is hardly any force of attraction between particles in gases. ☐

Particles in liquids are held in fixed positions by strong forces. ☐

---

1 A chemical can undergo a physical change when it changes temperature. **Grade 4-6**
It can also undergo a chemical change when reacted with other substances.

Describe the differences between a physical change and a chemical change.
Give your answer in terms of the end product.

....

....

....

....

[Total 2 marks]

---

2 The particle model helps to describe the different states of matter. **Grade 6-7**

a) Give **two** limitations of the particle model.

....

....

[2]

b) Describe the differences between liquids and solids in terms of the movement of particles.

....

....

....

[2]

[Total 4 marks]

Changing State

1   This question is about the processes by which a material changes state.   Grade 4-6

a) What is the name of the process when a solid becomes a liquid?

....

[1]

b) What is the name of the temperature at which a liquid becomes a gas?

....

[1]

c) If a liquid turns into a gas at a very high temperature, what does this imply about the strength of the bonds between the particles in the substance?

....

[1]

[Total 3 marks]

2   Use the data in the table below to help you answer the questions that follow.   Grade 6-7

Substance	Sodium Chloride	Water	Copper
Melting Point (°C)	801	0	1083
Boiling Point (°C)	1413	100	2567

a) Which substance in the table would be a liquid at 900 °C?

....

[1]

b) Which two substances would be gases at 1500 °C?

....

[2]

c) Based on the information given in the table, which process requires the most energy: melting copper or boiling sodium chloride?

....

[1]

d) Does the data in the table suggest that the bonds between copper atoms are stronger than the bonds between water molecules? Explain your answer.

....

....

....

[2]

[Total 6 marks]

Chemical Formulas

Warm-Up

Using a periodic table, write the symbols of the following elements.

Boron: ....   Tin: ....   Manganese: ....   Chlorine: ....

1   Look at the diagram. It shows the displayed formula of the compound dithionic acid.

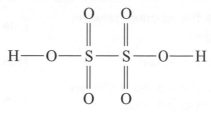

a) Name the elements present in this compound.

....
                                                                                                                        [2]

b) What is the molecular formula of this compound?
Give your answer in the form $H_aS_bO_c$, where a, b and c are whole numbers.

....
                                                                                                                        [1]

[Total 3 marks]

2   The following list contains a variety of substances identified by their chemical formula.

A. O_2 **B.** NaCl   **C.** C_2H_4 **D.** SO   **E.** H_2O **F.** SO_2

a) Name substance **E**.

....
                                                                                                                        [1]

b) How many atoms are there in a molecule of substance **C**?

....
                                                                                                                        [1]

c) Which **one** of the substances is sulfur monoxide?

....
                                                                                                                        [1]

d) Substance **B** is an ionic compound, whereas the other substances listed have simple
covalent structures. Describe the difference between the information given in the
formula of an ionic compound and the formula of a molecular compound.

....

....
                                                                                                                        [2]

[Total 5 marks]

Chemical Equations

The chemical word equation for a reaction is shown below.

magnesium + hydrochloric acid → magnesium chloride + hydrogen

For each of the following statements circle whether the statement is **true** or **false**.

1)	Hydrogen is a product in the reaction	True	Or	False
2)	The equation shows the reaction between chlorine and hydrogen	True	Or	False
3)	Hydrochloric acid is a reactant	True	Or	False
4)	The equation shows the reaction between magnesium and hydrochloric acid	True	Or	False

1   Potassium (K) reacts vigorously with chlorine gas (Cl_2) to form potassium chloride (KCl) only.

a) Write a word equation for this reaction.

....

[1]

b) Which of the following equations correctly represents this reaction?
Place a tick (✓) in the box next to the correct answer.

$K + Cl → KCl$ ☐ $K_2 + 2Cl → 2KCl$ ☐

$K_2 + Cl_2 → 2KCl$ ☐ $2K + Cl_2 → 2KCl$ ☐

[1]

[Total 2 marks]

2   Hydrogen gas is an important reactant, used in the Haber process. It can be made, at high temperatures, using the following reaction.

$$CH_4 + H_2O → CO + 3H_2$$

Which of the following word equations correctly describes this reaction?
Place a tick (✓) in the box next to the correct answer.

methane + steam → carbon dioxide + hydrogen   ☐

ethane + steam → carbon dioxide + hydrogen   ☐

methane + steam → carbon monoxide + hydrogen   ☐

methane + steam → carbon + oxygen + hydrogen   ☐

[Total 1 mark]

3 Sodium metal can react with oxygen molecules in the air to form sodium oxide (Na_2O). *Grade 4-6*

Write a balanced equation for this reaction.

....
[Total 2 marks]

4 Nitric acid can be made using ammonia. *Grade 6-7*

a) The first stage in the manufacture of nitric acid is to oxidise ammonia, NH_3, to nitrogen(II) oxide, NO. Balance the equation for the reaction.

.... NH_3 + ... O_2 → .... NO + ... H_2O

[1]

b) The reaction below shows the final stage in the manufacture of nitric acid. The equation is not balanced correctly. Explain how you can tell.

$$2NO_2 + O_2 + H_2O \rightarrow 2HNO_3$$

....

....

[1]

[Total 2 marks]

5 In a chemical reaction, sulfuric acid and aluminium metal react to form hydrogen gas and a salt solution of aluminium sulfate. *Grade 6-7*

Ben has written this equation for the reaction:

$$Al_{(s)} + H_2SO_{4 (aq)} \rightarrow Al_2(SO_4)_{3 (aq)} + H_{2 (g)}$$

Ben's equation is not balanced. Write a balanced chemical equation for this reaction.

....
[Total 2 marks]

6 Balance the following symbol equation to show how sulfur reacts with nitric acid. *Grade 7-9*

$$S + HNO_3 \rightarrow H_2SO_4 + NO_2 + H_2O$$

....
[Total 2 marks]

Chapter C1 — Air and Water

Endothermic and Exothermic Reactions

1 Which of the following energy changes could be the result of an exothermic reaction?

Place a tick (✓) in the box next to the correct answer.

	Energy of products	Temperature of surroundings
A	Greater than reactants	Increases
B	Less than reactants	Increases
C	Greater than reactants	Decreases
D	Less than reactants	Decreases

A ☐   **B** ☐   **C** ☐   **D** ☐

[Total 1 mark]

2 The reaction between ethanoic acid and sodium carbonate is an endothermic reaction.

Sketch a reaction profile for this reaction on the axes below.
Label the reactants, the products and the activation energy.

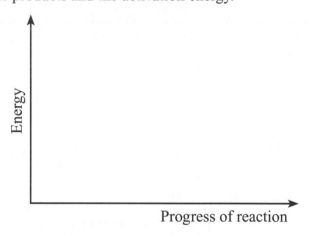

[Total 3 marks]

3 A company is trying to find a reaction with a low activation energy to use in a hand warmer.
The reaction profiles for the reactions being investigated are shown below.
The scale on the energy axis is the same for each reaction profile.

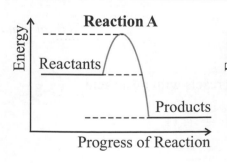
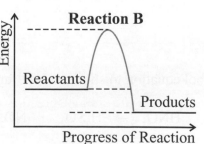
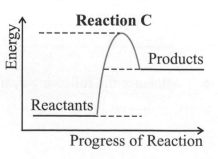

Suggest which reaction would be most suitable for using in a hand warmer. Explain your answer.

....

....

....

[Total 3 marks]

Chapter C1 — Air and Water   ☐   ☐   ☐

Measuring Temperature Changes

1   A student is investigating the temperature change that occurs when he dissolves the same number of moles of two different salts, **A** and **B**, in water.

Grade 6-7

a) Suggest **three** essential pieces of apparatus needed for the investigation.

....

....
[3]

b)*Describe a method that the student could use to carry out his investigation. Include details of any variables that would need to be controlled.

....

....

....

....

....

....

....

....

....
[6]

c) The student's results are shown in the table below. Complete the table.

Salt	Initial temperature (°C)	End temperature (°C)	Temperature change (°C)
A	21.0	16.0	....
B	21.0	26.5	....

[2]

d) Which of the statements below about the student's results is correct? Place a tick (✓) in the box next to the correct answer.

☐ Both salts dissolved exothermically.

☐ Salt A dissolved exothermically, but salt B dissolved endothermically.

☐ Salt A dissolved endothermically, but salt B dissolved exothermically.

☐ Both salts dissolved endothermically.

[1]

[Total 12 marks]

Chapter C1 — Air and Water

Bond Energies

Which of the following statements is true?
Place a tick (✓) in the box next to the correct answer.

☐ During exothermic reactions, the energy taken to break the bonds in the reactants is greater than the energy released by making the bonds in the products.

☐ During endothermic reactions, the energy released by breaking bonds in the reactants is less than the energy taken to make the bonds in the products.

☐ During exothermic reactions, the energy taken to break the bonds in the reactants is less than the energy released by making the bonds in the products.

☐ During endothermic reactions, the energy taken to break the bonds in the reactants is less than the energy released by making the bonds in the products.

1 Look at the table below. It shows the bond energies of some bonds.

Bond	Bond energy (kJ/mol)
C — H	413
C — O	358
H — O	463
C = C	614
C — C	347

a) Use the table to work out the energy change of the following reaction between ethene and water.

$$\underset{H}{\overset{H}{\diagdown}}C=C\underset{H}{\overset{H}{\diagup}} \quad + \quad \underset{H}{\overset{O}{\diagdown}}H \quad \rightarrow \quad H-\underset{\underset{H}{|}}{\overset{\overset{H}{|}}{C}}-\underset{\underset{H}{|}}{\overset{\overset{H}{|}}{C}}-O-H$$

.... kJ/mol

[3]

b) Use your answer to a) to deduce whether the reaction between ethene and water is endothermic or exothermic. Explain your answer.

....

....

[2]

[Total 5 marks]

2 The energy change of the following reaction is –119 kJ/mol.

$$H-\underset{\underset{H}{|}}{\overset{\overset{H}{|}}{C}}-\underset{\underset{H}{|}}{\overset{\overset{H}{|}}{C}}-H \ + \ Cl-Cl \quad \rightarrow \quad H-\underset{\underset{H}{|}}{\overset{\overset{H}{|}}{C}}-\underset{\underset{H}{|}}{\overset{\overset{Cl}{|}}{C}}-H \ + \ H-Cl$$

a) Is the reaction endothermic or exothermic?

....

[1]

b) Use this information, as well as the data in the table,
to work out the approximate bond energy of an H—Cl bond.

Bond	Bond energy (kJ/mol)
C — H	413
C — C	347
C — Cl	339
Cl — Cl	239

.... kJ/mol
[3]

c) Use your answer from b) to rank the H—Cl bond and the bonds
from the table in order of strength, from weakest to strongest.

....

[1]

[Total 5 marks]

Exam Practice Tip

In questions involving calculating energy changes from bond energies (or vice versa), it can be really useful to draw out the <u>displayed formulas</u> of any chemicals you're dealing with (unless you're given them in the question o' course). Displayed formulas show all the atoms and all the bonds between them, and make it easy to see what bonds have broken and what new bonds have been made during a chemical reaction.

The Evolution of the Atmosphere

1 Which of these statements about Earth's early atmosphere is **correct**? Grade 4-6

Place a tick (✓) in the box next to the correct answer.

Most of the gases that made up Earth's early atmosphere were released by volcanic eruptions. ☐

The Earth's oceans were formed when the methane in the early atmosphere condensed. ☐

Earth's early atmosphere contained less carbon dioxide than the atmosphere today. ☐

Earth's early atmosphere contained a lot of oxygen. ☐

[Total 1 mark]

2 Scientists have looked at the composition of other planets to provide evidence for what the early atmosphere on Earth was like. The table below shows the compositions of the atmospheres on Mars and Earth. Grade 7-9

	Percentage composition (%)					
	H_2O	Ne	CO_2	N_2	O_2	Ar
Mars	0.030	trace	95	2.7	0.13	1.6
Earth	0–4.0	0.0018	0.036	78	21	0.93

a) i) Scientists believe Earth's early atmosphere was similar to the atmosphere on Mars today. Using the table, suggest which gas made up the majority of Earth's early atmosphere.

....
[1]

ii) Explain **two** ways in which this gas was removed from Earth's atmosphere as it evolved.

....

....
[2]

b) Explain how oxygen built up in Earth's atmosphere and suggest why there is hardly any oxygen present in the atmosphere on Mars.

....

....

....
[2]

c) Which gas is present in the **highest** concentration in the Earth's atmosphere today?

....
[1]

[Total 6 marks]

Combustion and Air Pollution

1 A variety of pollutants can be released when fuels burn, with a range of consequences. [Grade 4-6]

a) When a hydrocarbon combusts, hydrogen and carbon gain oxygen.
What is the name given to reactions where reactants gain oxygen?

....

[1]

b) Some pollutants form as a result of a fuel combusting incompletely.
Under what circumstances will incomplete combustion occur?

....

[1]

c) Give **one** effect that the following products of incomplete combustion could have on health:

i) Carbon monoxide: ....

ii) Carbon particulates: ....

[2]

[Total 4 marks]

2 The table below shows the concentration of pollutants in two cities, **A** and **B**. [Grade 6-7]

City	Concentration of Pollutants ($\mu g/m^3$)		
	Nitrogen dioxide	Particulate carbon	Sulfur dioxide
A	13.2	65.1	8.9
B	106.4	13.2	68.2

a) In one city, the buildings have become covered with a black powder.
Suggest which city this has happened in and why it has occurred.

....

....

[2]

b) Buildings in one of the cities have become damaged as a result of chemical weathering.
Which of the cities, **A** or **B**, is this likely to have occurred in?
Explain your answer using evidence from the table.

....

....

....

[2]

c) Suggest **two** things that could be done to reduce the amounts of these pollutants in cities.

....

....

[2]

[Total 6 marks]

Chapter C1 — Air and Water

Greenhouse Gases and Climate Change

1 Greenhouse gases in the atmosphere help maintain life on Earth. (Grade 4-6)

a) Which of the following is **not** a greenhouse gas?
Place a tick (✓) in the box next to the correct answer.

Carbon dioxide ☐   Methane ☐

Nitrogen ☐   Water vapour ☐

[1]

b) State how greenhouse gases help to support life on Earth.

....

[1]

[Total 2 marks]

2 Many scientists believe that increased levels of greenhouse gases, such as carbon dioxide, have resulted in global warming. (Grade 6-7)

a) Give the definition of a greenhouse gas.

....

....

[1]

b) Elvis states the following:

> Any greenhouse effect is dangerous as it could cause global warming.

Is Elvis correct? Explain your answer.

....

....

....

[1]

c) Global warming is a type of climate change.
Give **two** environmental consequences associated with global warming.

....

....

[2]

d) Give **one** reason why it's difficult to make predictions about climate change.

....

[1]

[Total 5 marks]

3* The graph below shows how both the global temperature anomaly (the difference between current temperature and an average value) and the concentration of CO_2 in the atmosphere have varied over time. Describe the trends in the data and suggest reasons for them.

....

....

....

....

....

....

[Total 6 marks]

4 The graph below shows CO_2 emissions by fossil fuels in the UK and the changes in sea levels between 1993 and 2013.

A scientist concludes that, since sea levels have risen despite CO_2 emissions decreasing, human activities are not the cause of rising global sea levels. State whether the scientist's conclusions are valid. Explain your answer.

....

....

....

....

[Total 4 marks]

Chapter C1 — Air and Water

Reducing Pollution

1 In recent years, some businesses have tried to make their operations carbon neutral. *Grade 6-7*

a) Explain the term 'carbon neutral'.

....

[1]

b) Suggest **two** methods a business could use to offset its carbon footprint.

....

....

[2]

c) Governments can tax companies based on their greenhouse gas emissions or put a cap on the emissions a company can produce. Discuss why some countries may be resistant to using these methods.

....

....

....

[2]

[Total 5 marks]

2 One way to reduce air pollution is by using carbon capture. There are benefits and risks to this method. *Grade 6-7*

a) Explain how carbon capture can be used to reduce air pollution.

....

....

[2]

b) State **one** disadvantage of using carbon capture at a power station.

....

....

[1]

c) Shona states that as well as carbon capture, other methods also need to be developed to reduce greenhouse gas emissions. Explain why this is.

....

....

[1]

[Total 4 marks]

Exam Practice Tip

Learning the definitions for all the different terms that crop up in GCSE chemistry may be a bit of a bore, but it might be really useful in the exams. Learning all the itty bitty details is worth it if it means you get all the marks available.

Tests for Gases

1 Amelia is testing for gases.

The diagram below shows a gas being tested.

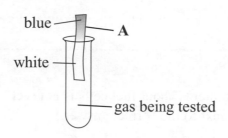

blue —— A
white ——
—— gas being tested

a) Identify the item labelled **A** in the diagram.

....

[1]

b) Suggest which gas was present in the test tube.

....

[1]

[Total 2 marks]

2 Vicky performs an experiment that produces a colourless gas. Vicky does not know what the gas is, so she collects it and tests it in order to identify it. *(Grade 6-7)*

a) Suggest why Vicky should perform the experiment in a fume cupboard.

....

[1]

b) Describe how Vicky could test the gas to see if it was carbon dioxide.

....

....

[2]

c) When Vicky placed a lighted splint into a sample of the gas, it was **not** accompanied by a popping sound. What does this tell you about the gas she had collected?

....

[1]

d) When Vicky placed a glowing splint into a sample of the gas, the splint relighted. Identify the gas that was produced by her experiment.

....

[1]

[Total 5 marks]

Chapter C1 — Air and Water

Fuel Cells

1 Fuel cells are an alternative way of producing energy, instead of burning crude oil. **Grade 6-7**

a) Define the term 'fuel cell'.

....

....

[2]

b) Which of the following statements about fuel cells is **correct**?
Place a tick (✓) in the box next to the correct answer.

Fuel cells produce a potential difference indefinitely. ☐

Fuel cells produce a potential difference until the reactants are completely used up. ☐

Fuel cells start to produce a potential difference once all the reactants are used up. ☐

Fuel cells produce a potential difference until the reactants are partly used up. ☐

[1]

[Total 3 marks]

2 George is investigating the advantages and disadvantages of hydrogen-oxygen fuel cells. **Grade 7-9**

a) Explain why using hydrogen as a fuel instead of petrol might still require the use of fossil fuels.

....

....

....

[2]

b) Give **one** other disadvantage of using hydrogen-oxygen fuel cells to power cars.

....

....

[1]

c) George states that we shouldn't use hydrogen-oxygen fuel cells as
they produce harmful waste chemicals. Comment on George's answer,
with reference to any chemical produced by hydrogen-oxygen fuel cells.

....

....

[2]

[Total 5 marks]

Exam Practice Tip

You might get an exam question about the advantages and disadvantages of using fuel cells for a particular purpose.
Make sure you think carefully about your answer — some advantages and disadvantages only apply to certain uses.

Potable Water

1 Which of the following is **not** a correct description of potable water? (Grade 4-6)

Place a tick (✓) in the box next to the incorrect description.

Pure water. ☐   Water that has been treated. ☐

Water that is safe to drink. ☐   Water with a low concentration of salt. ☐

[Total 1 mark]

2 A purification plant uses multiple steps to purify water. (Grade 6-7)

a) When the water arrives at a water purification plant, any solid impurities are removed. Give the name of this step.

....
[1]

b) The purification process ends with chlorination. Explain what happens during this process.

....
....
[1]

[Total 2 marks]

3 The way that countries source their water is dependent on a variety of factors. The table below shows the average annual rainfall in the UK and Kuwait. (Grade 6-7)

Country	Average annual rainfall (mm)
UK	1129
Kuwait	120

a) One of these countries gets large quantities of its water by distilling seawater. Suggest which country and explain your answer.

....
....
....
[2]

b) Give **one** disadvantage of using this process to purify large quantities of drinking water.

....
[1]

c) Other than distillation, state **one** other method that can be used to make seawater potable.

....
[1]

[Total 4 marks]

The History of the Atom

Warm-Up

Draw **one** line from each stage of atomic model development to the correct description of that model.

Stage of Atomic Model Development

Plum pudding model

Ancient Greek model

Rutherford's nuclear model

Description

A positively charged 'ball' with negatively charged electrons in it.

A small, positively charged nucleus surrounded by a 'cloud' of negative electrons.

Everything is made up of four elements — earth, air, fire and water.

1 Models of the atom have changed over time. **Grade 4-6**

Which of the following statements is the best description of what scientists thought atoms were like before the electron was discovered?
Place a tick (✓) in the box next to the correct answer.

Tiny solid spheres that □   Formless 'clouds' □   Flat geometric □   Discrete packets □
can't be divided.   of matter.   shapes.   of energy.

[Total 1 mark]

2 Over time, scientists have conducted experiments which have led to the development of the atomic model. Two of these scientists were J J Thomson and Ernest Rutherford. **Grade 7-9**

a) Thomson's experiments led to the discovery of the electron. He realised that there must be positive charge in an atom as well as the negative charge of the electrons. Suggest how Thomson could have worked this out using his knowledge of the atom and its charge.

....

....

[2]

b) Rutherford devised the gold foil experiment where positively charged alpha particles were fired at gold foil. He predicted that most of the particles would pass straight through the foil and a few might be deflected slightly. Describe what actually happened to the alpha particles during the gold foil experiment and explain why it happened.

....

....

....

....

[4]

[Total 6 marks]

The Atom

1   The diagram below shows the structure of a helium atom.

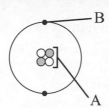

a)   Name the subatomic particles in region **A** and give their relative charges.

....

....

                [2]

b)   What is the relative charge of subatomic particle **B**?

....

                [1]

c)   Roughly how big is region **A** compared to the diameter of the atom?
     Place a tick (✓) in the box next to the correct answer.

one hundred-thousandth of the atomic diameter   ☐   one thousandth of the atomic diameter   ☐

one ten-millionth of the atomic diameter   ☐   one hundredth of the atomic diameter   ☐

                [1]

           [Total 4 marks]

2   An atom has a diameter of approximately 10^{-10} m.

a)   Which of the following is closest to the diameter of an atom in size?
     Place a tick (✓) in the box next to the correct answer.

The radius of a nucleus.   ☐

The width of a grain of sand.   ☐

The length of a chemical bond.   ☐

The diameter of a nanoparticle.   ☐

                [1]

b)   Explain how the movement of electrons determines the size of an atom.

....

....

....

                [2]

           [Total 3 marks]

 ☐   ☐   ☐

Chapter C2 — Chemical Patterns

Atoms, Ions and Isotopes

1 Ions can have either a positive or a negative charge. **Grade 4-6**

   a) Describe what happens to an atom when it turns into a negative ion.

   ....

                                                [1]

   b) Magnesium has an atomic number of 12.
      Calculate the number of electrons found in one Mg^{2+} ion.

                                        Number of electrons = ...

                                                [1]

                                      [Total 2 marks]

2 This question is about isotopes. **Grade 6-7**

   a) A neutral atom of sulfur, ^{32}S, has 16 electrons. Sulfur has three other
      naturally occurring isotopes, with mass numbers 33, 34 and 36.
      Complete the table below, giving the number of protons, neutrons
      and electrons for each of the naturally occurring isotopes of sulfur.

Isotope	Number of Protons	Number of Neutrons	Number of Electrons
^{32}S	....	....	16
^{33}S	....	....	....
^{34}S	....	....	....
^{36}S	....	....	....

                                                [3]

   b) Atom **X** has a mass number of 51 and an atomic number of 23.
      Atom **Y** has a mass number of 51 and an atomic number of 22.
      Atom **Z** has a mass number of 52 and an atomic number of 23.

      Identify which pair of atoms are isotopes and explain why.

   ....

   ....

   ....

                                                [3]

                                      [Total 6 marks]

Exam Practice Tip

Don't let isotopes confuse you. Just because they've got different numbers of neutrons, a pair of isotopes will still have the same number of protons and electrons, so they're still the same element — they just have a different mass number.

Chapter C2 — Chemical Patterns

The Periodic Table

1 Chemical elements are arranged in the periodic table. **Grade 4-6**

a) How are the elements ordered in the modern periodic table?

....

[1]

b) Place a tick (✓) in the box that tells you how the elements in Period 4
of the periodic table compare to the elements in Period 3.

Elements in Period 4 have one less
shell of electrons than elements in ☐
Period 3 that are in the same group.

Elements in Period 4 have one less
electron in their outer shell than elements ☐
in Period 3 that are in the same group.

Elements in Period 4 have one more
shell of electrons than elements in ☐
Period 3 that are in the same group.

Elements in Period 4 have one more
electron in their outer shell than elements ☐
in Period 3 that are in the same group.

[1]

[Total 2 marks]

2 Mendeleev created an early version of the periodic table, in which he arranged the elements
according to their atomic masses and their properties. Mendeleev left some gaps in his table. **Grade 7-9**

a) Why did Mendeleev decide to leave gaps and switch the position of some elements?

....

....

[1]

b) One of the gaps that Mendeleev left was in Group 4. He predicted that there was
an undiscovered element that would fit in this position of the table. He called this
element **eka-silicon**. The table below shows some properties of the Group 4
elements silicon and tin, plus some predictions about the properties of eka-silicon.

	Silicon (Si)	Eka-silicon (Ek)	Tin (Sn)
Atomic Mass	28	72	119
Appearance	grey/silver non-metal	grey metal	grey metal
Formula of chloride	$SiCl_4$	?	$SnCl_4$

Use the information in the table to predict the formula of eka-silicon chloride.

....

[1]

c) Describe how the discovery of new elements in the years after
Mendeleev published his table supported his decision to leave gaps.

....

....

....

[1]

[Total 3 marks]

Electronic Structure

1   The atomic number of neon is 10.   (Grade 4-6)

How many electrons does neon have in its **outer shell**?
Place a tick (✓) in the box next to the correct answer.

2 ☐   6 ☐   8 ☐   10 ☐

[Total 1 mark]

2   The atomic number of sulfur is 16.   (Grade 6-7)

a)   Write down the electronic structure of sulfur.

....

[1]

b)   Draw a diagram to show how the electrons are arranged in a single sulfur atom.

[1]

[Total 2 marks]

3   Magnesium is found in Group 2 and Period 3 of the periodic table.   (Grade 6-7)

a)   Use the periodic table to determine which of the following elements will react in a
similar way to magnesium. Place a tick (✓) in the box next to the correct answer.

Si ☐   Be ☐   Li ☐   S ☐

[1]

b)   Explain how you could use the position of magnesium in the periodic table to **deduce** its
electronic structure. Give the electronic structure of magnesium as part of your answer.

....

....

....

....

[4]

[Total 5 marks]

Metals and Non-Metals

1   Metals make up about 80% of all the elements in the periodic table. **Grade 4-6**
    Aluminium and magnesium are both metals.

a) Describe where metals and non-metals can be found in the periodic table.

Metals: ....

Non-metals: ....

[1]

b) Which of the statements below is **true**? Place a tick (✓) in the box next to the correct answer.

Elements that react to form negative ions are metals. ☐

Elements that react to form positive ions are metals. ☐

Elements that react to form positive ions are non-metals. ☐

Elements that do not form ions are metals. ☐

[1]

c) Name **two** types of chemical bond that magnesium or aluminium could form.

....

[2]

d) Explain why magnesium and aluminium react in a similar way.

....

....

[2]

[Total 6 marks]

2   Iron is a transition metal. It can react with sulfur, a non-metal, to form iron sulfide. **Grade 6-7**

a) Using your knowledge of typical metals and non-metals,
    compare the physical properties of iron and sulfur.

....

....

....

[4]

b) Many transition elements can form coloured compounds.
    Give **two** other properties that are specific to transition metals.

....

[2]

c) Name **two** transition metals, other than iron.

....

[2]

[Total 8 marks]

Chapter C2 — Chemical Patterns

Group 1 Elements

Place a tick (✓) in the correct box next to each of the statements.

Statement	True	False
Group 1 elements are non-metals.		
Group 1 metals tarnish in moist air.		
Density decreases as you go down Group 1.		
Group 1 metals get harder down the group.		
Lithium is less dense than water.		
Storing sodium in oil prevents it from tarnishing.		

1   In the reaction between potassium and water, two products are formed.
Place a tick (✓) in the **two** boxes next to the correct products.

Grade 4-6

potassium hydroxide ☐   oxygen ☐

carbon dioxide ☐   hydrogen ☐

potassium chloride ☐   potassium oxide ☐

[Total 2 marks]

2   The Group 1 elements have relatively low melting and boiling points.
They react readily to form ionic compounds. Their ions usually have a charge of 1+.

Grade 6-7

a)   Explain why the elements in Group 1 usually form 1+ ions.

    ....

    ....

[2]

b)   The table below shows information about the melting
and boiling points of the first three Group 1 elements.

Element	Melting point (°C)	Boiling point (°C)
Lithium	181	1342
Sodium	....	883
Potassium	63	759

Use the information in the table to predict the melting point of sodium.
Put your answer in the table.   [1]

[Total 3 marks]

3 Alex is investigating the reactions of Group 1 elements with different reactants. Grade 6-7

a) i) Alex reacts lithium with chlorine. A vigorous reaction occurs which produces a white crystalline salt. Name the salt that is formed.

....

[1]

ii) Write a balanced symbol equation for this reaction. Include state symbols in your answer.

....

[3]

b) He repeats the experiment with potassium. Name the product of the reaction between potassium and chlorine and explain why potassium and lithium both react with chlorine in a similar way.

....

....

....

[2]

c) Alex adds a piece of sodium to some water and times how long it takes for the sodium to disappear. He then repeats the experiment with metal **A**, another Group 1 metal. The two pieces of metal he uses have the same mass and surface area. Metal **A** takes more time to disappear than the sodium. Which Group 1 metal is metal **A**? Explain your answer.

....

....

....

[3]

[Total 9 marks]

4 The element francium is below caesium in Group 1 of the periodic table. Despite being a rare and unstable element, we can still make predictions about francium's reactivity. Grade 7-9

a) Compare the reactivity of francium to caesium.
Justify your answer using your knowledge of francium's electron arrangement.

....

....

....

[3]

b) Group 1 elements react with phosphorus, P_4, to form ionic phosphides. Lithium reacts with phosphorus to form lithium phosphide Li_3P. Predict the formula of francium phosphide and write a balanced equation for the reaction of phosphorus and francium.

Formula: ....

Equation: ....

[3]

[Total 6 marks]

Chapter C2 — Chemical Patterns

Group 7 Elements

1 The elements in Group 7 of the periodic table are known as the halogens. (Grade 4-6)

Place a tick (✓) in the boxes next to the **two** statements that are **true**.

Group 7 elements are metals that exist as single atoms. ☐

Fluorine is a dark grey solid at room temperature. ☐

Halogens are non-metals that exist as molecules of two atoms. ☐

The melting points of Group 7 elements decrease down the group. ☐

Chlorine is a green gas at room temperature. ☐

[Total 2 marks]

2 The halogens can react with alkali metals to form metal halide salts. (Grade 4-6)

a) Name the metal halide salt that will be formed when bromine and sodium react.

....

[1]

b) When fluorine gas reacts with potassium, the salt potassium fluoride, KF, is formed.
Write the balanced symbol equation for this reaction. Include state symbols in your answer.

....

[3]

[Total 4 marks]

3 The reactivity of Group 7 elements is dependent on their electronic configuration. (Grade 7-9)

a) Describe the electronic configuration of Group 7 elements and how it changes down the group.

....

....

....

[2]

b) At room temperature, sodium reacts violently with fluorine to form sodium fluoride.
Give **one** similarity and **one** difference between the reaction of sodium and fluorine
and the reaction that would occur between sodium and iodine. Explain your answer.

....

....

....

....

....

[4]

[Total 6 marks]

Chapter C2 — Chemical Patterns

PRACTICAL

4   Josie investigated the reactions that occur when chlorine, bromine or iodine are
     added to different sodium halide solutions. The table below shows her results.

	Sodium chloride solution ($NaCl_{(aq)}$, colourless)	Sodium bromide solution ($NaBr_{(aq)}$, colourless)	Sodium iodide solution ($NaI_{(aq)}$, colourless)
Add chlorine water ($Cl_{2\,(aq)}$, colourless)	no reaction	solution turns orange	....
Add bromine water ($Br_{2\,(aq)}$, orange)	no reaction	....	solution turns brown
Add iodine water ($I_{2\,(aq)}$, brown)	no reaction	no reaction	no reaction

a) Use your knowledge of the reactivity trend of the
    halogens to fill in the missing results in the table.

                                                                        [2]

b) Explain why there was no reaction when Josie added iodine water to sodium bromide solution.

    ....

    ....
                                                                        [2]

c) Construct a balanced symbol equation for the reaction that happened
    when Josie added chlorine water to sodium bromide solution.

    ....
                                                                        [2]

d) Astatine is below iodine in Group 7. Although astatine is rare and breaks down
    easily, we can still make predictions about its reactivity. Predict whether chlorine
    water would react with sodium astatide solution. Explain your answer.

    ....

    ....
                                                                        [2]
                                                              [Total 8 marks]

Exam Practice Tip

One of the most important things to learn about Group 7 elements is the trend you find in reactivity as you go down or
up the group. And you need to be able to explain this trend using the electronic structure of the halogens. Smashing.

Chapter C2 — Chemical Patterns

Group 0 Elements

1 Place a tick (✓) in the box next to the statement that is **true** for the noble gases. **Grade 4-6**

They are colourful gases. ☐   They have only 1 electron in their outer shells. ☐

They are monatomic. ☐   They react with alkali metals to form salts. ☐

[Total 1 mark]

2 When welders join two metals together, the metals are heated to a very high temperature and argon gas is blown over the hot weld. In the absence of argon, gases in the air would react with the hot, molten metal, forming compounds that make joining more difficult. **Grade 6-7**

Explain why argon is suitable for this use, including ideas about electronic structure.

....

....

....

....

[Total 3 marks]

3 The noble gases are inert gases that make up Group 0 of the periodic table. **Grade 6-7**

The table below shows some information about the first four noble gases.

Element	Symbol	Boiling point (°C)	Density (kg/m³)
Helium	He	−269	0.18
Neon	Ne	−246	0.90
Argon	Ar	−186	?
Krypton	Kr	−153	3.7

a) The element below krypton in Group 0 is xenon.
   Use the information in the table to predict what the boiling point of xenon will be.

boiling point = ... °C
[1]

b) Use the information in the table to predict the density of argon.

density = ... kg/m³
[1]

[Total 2 marks]

Exam Practice Tip

Make sure you get lots of practice at questions like Q3, where you're given information about some of the elements in a group and asked to use it to predict something about another element in the group. They need thinking through carefully.

Chapter C2 — Chemical Patterns

Ionic Compounds

Choose from the formulas on the left to complete the table showing the dot and cross diagrams and formulas of various ionic compounds. You won't need to use all the formulas.

NaCl   MgCl$_2$ MgCl

Na$_2$O   NaO   NaCl$_2$

Dot and cross diagram	Chemical formula
[Na]$^+$ [Cl]$^-$	
[Na]$^+$ [O]$^{2-}$ [Na]$^+$	
[Cl]$^-$ [Mg]$^{2+}$ [Cl]$^-$	

1 Ionic bonding is one of the three types of chemical bond that elements can form.

In which of the following compounds are the particles held together by ionic bonds? Place a tick (✓) in the boxes next to the **two** compounds that you think are ionic.

calcium chloride ☐   carbon dioxide ☐   phosphorus trichloride ☐

potassium oxide ☐   nitrogen monoxide ☐

[Total 2 marks]

2 Calcium fluoride is an ionic compound.

a) What is the chemical formula for calcium fluoride?

....

[1]

b) Draw a dot and cross diagram to show the bonding in calcium fluoride. You should include the charges on the ions in your diagram.

[3]

[Total 4 marks]

3 Ionic compounds are formed from anions and cations.

The table below shows the details of four different ionic compounds.

a) Complete the table.

Ionic Compound	Cation	Anion	Chemical Formula	Melting Point (°C)
Calcium chloride	....	Cl^-	$CaCl_2$	772
Barium nitrate	Ba^{2+}	NO_3^-	....	592
Potassium carbonate	K^+	CO_3^{2-}	....	891
Lithium oxide	Li^+	....	Li_2O	1438

[4]

b) Carbon monoxide is an oxygen-containing covalent molecule with a melting point of –205 °C.
Lithium oxide also contains oxygen but has a much higher melting point.
Explain what causes the significantly higher melting point of lithium oxide.

....

....

....

....

[2]

[Total 6 marks]

4 Beryllium sulfide is an ionic compound.

a) Give the chemical formula of beryllium sulfide.

....

[1]

b) Describe the structure of a crystal of beryllium sulfide. You should state:
 • What particles are present in the crystal.
 • How these particles are arranged.
 • What holds the particles together.

....

....

....

....

[4]

[Total 5 marks]

5 The table below shows some data about sodium fluoride. Explain how the structure of sodium fluoride determines each of the four properties shown in the table.

Boiling point (°C)	Electrical conductivity of solid	Electrical conductivity of solution	Soluble in water?
1695	Low	High	Yes

Boiling point ....

....

Electrical conductivity of solid ....

....

Electrical conductivity of solution ....

....

Solubility in water ....

....

[Total 7 marks]

6 The diagram below shows a ball and stick model of an ionic compound.

a) Draw the corresponding dot and cross diagram for this ionic compound.

[3]

b) What is the empirical formula of this compound?

....

[1]

c)* Discuss the uses and limitations of dot and cross diagrams.

....

....

....

....

....

[6]

[Total 10 marks]

Chapter C2 — Chemical Patterns

Metallic Bonding and Reactivity

Warm-Up

Which of the following are typical properties of a metal? Circle the correct answers.

good conductor of heat   brittle   high melting point   low density   malleable

low boiling point   poor conductor of electricity   crystal structure when solid

1 Metals react in similar ways, and can be placed in order of their reactivity. *(Grade 4-6)*

Place a tick (✓) in the box next to the statement that is **incorrect**.

The easier it is for a metal atom to form a positive ion, the less reactive it will be.   ☐

Metals generally react by losing electrons.   ☐

Metals are able to form ionic compounds.   ☐

In a reactivity series, you will find a reactive metal above a less reactive metal.   ☐

[Total 1 mark]

2 Many properties of solid metals are due to their structure. *(Grade 6-7)*

a) Draw and label a diagram to show the structure of a solid metal.

[3]

b) i) Explain how this structure means metals usually have high melting points.

....

....

....

[2]

ii) Explain how this structure allows solid metals to conduct electricity.

....

....

....

[2]

[Total 7 marks]

Exam Practice Tip

Knowing the reactivity series could be really useful when it comes to answering questions in the exams. Try learning this mnemonic to help you remember... <u>P</u>urple <u>S</u>oap <u>Ca</u>n <u>M</u>ake <u>A</u>unty <u>Z</u>ainab's <u>I</u>guana <u>L</u>ilac — <u>H</u>ow <u>C</u>olourfully <u>S</u>illy. (You don't have to use my Booker Prize winning concoction, though. You could also make up your own.)

Ionic Equations and Reactions of Metals

1 Silver chloride, AgCl, can be made by reacting silver nitrate, AgNO₃, and sodium chloride, NaCl, together in a precipitation reaction.

$$AgNO_{3\,(aq)} + NaCl_{(aq)} \rightarrow AgCl_{(s)} + NaNO_{3\,(aq)}$$

Write a balanced ionic equation for the reaction above.

....

[Total 2 marks]

2 Shaun adds small pieces of some metals to metal salt solutions and leaves them for one hour. He records whether or not any reaction has taken place. His table of results is shown below.

	Magnesium	Silver	Aluminium	Lead
Magnesium chloride	no reaction	no reaction	no reaction	no reaction
Silver nitrate	magnesium nitrate and silver formed	no reaction	aluminium nitrate and silver formed	lead nitrate and silver formed
Aluminium chloride	magnesium chloride and aluminium formed	no reaction	no reaction	no reaction
Lead nitrate	magnesium nitrate and lead formed	no reaction	aluminium nitrate and lead formed	no reaction

a) Shaun says "My results show that lead is more reactive than silver." Do you agree? Explain your answer.

....

....

[1]

b) Construct a balanced symbol equation for the reaction between magnesium and aluminium chloride, AlCl₃.

....

[2]

c) Nickel is above lead in the reactivity series. Nickel is a shiny grey metal and nickel nitrate is green in solution. Lead is a dull grey metal and lead nitrate is colourless in solution. Suggest what Shaun would observe if he added nickel to lead nitrate solution.

....

....

....

[2]

[Total 5 marks]

        Chapter C3 — Chemicals of the Natural Environment

More Reactions of Metals

1 Amal performed some experiments to investigate the reactivity of metals.

a) First, Amal placed pieces of four different metals into dilute hydrochloric acid.
The diagram below shows what the four experiments looked like after 1 minute.

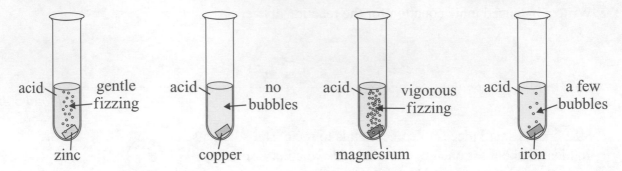

Use the information in the diagram to put these metals in order of reactivity.

Most reactive: ....

....

....

Least reactive: ....

[2]

b) Next, Amal was given samples of three mystery metals, marked **X**, **Y** and **Z**. She put small pieces of each of the metals in cold water. If there was no reaction with cold water, she tested the metal to see if it would react with steam. Her results are shown in the table below.

Metal	Any reaction with cold water?	Any reaction with steam?
X	Reacts vigorously. Hydrogen gas is produced.	
Y	no reaction	Reacts vigorously. Metal is coated with a white solid. Hydrogen gas is produced.
Z	no reaction	no reaction

i) Metal **Y** was zinc. It reacted with the steam to produce hydrogen gas and a white solid. Name the white solid that was produced by this reaction.

....

[1]

ii) One of the other metals Amal was given was sodium.
Suggest whether sodium was metal **X** or metal **Z**. Give a reason for your answer.

....

....

[1]

[Total 4 marks]

Chapter C3 — Chemicals of the Natural Environment

2 A student investigated the reactions of some metals and found the results shown in the table below.

Reaction	Observation
Lithium + water	Very vigorous reaction with fizzing, lithium disappears
Calcium + water	Fizzing, calcium disappears
Magnesium + water	No fizzing, a few bubbles on the magnesium
Copper + water	No fizzing, no change to copper
Iron + water	No fizzing, no change to iron
Lithium + dilute acid	Very vigorous reaction with fizzing, lithium disappears
Magnesium + dilute acid	Fizzing, magnesium disappears
Zinc + dilute acid	Fizzing, zinc disappears
Copper + dilute acid	No fizzing, no change to copper

a) Write an ionic equation for the reaction between magnesium and dilute acid.

....

[2]

b) Use the results in the table, along with your knowledge of the general reaction between an acid and a metal, to explain whether lithium or magnesium forms positive ions more easily.

....

....

....

[3]

c) Predict what the student would have seen if they had added sodium to water.

....

....

[2]

d) Put the metals calcium, copper and lithium in order from most reactive to least reactive.

....

[1]

e) Explain why it would be difficult to decide the order of reactivity of magnesium and zinc using these experiments. Suggest an experiment that could be used to decide which is more reactive.

....

....

[2]

[Total 10 marks]

Chapter C3 — Chemicals of the Natural Environment

Extracting Metals

1 The method used to extract metals from their ores can be determined using the reactivity series. The reactivity series of some elements is shown below.

Potassium	K	Most Reactive
Calcium	Ca	
Aluminium	Al	
Carbon	C	
Zinc	Zn	
Tin	Sn	
Copper	Cu	Least Reactive

a) Suggest a process that could be used to extract tin from its ore in industry.

....

....

[1]

b) State **one** other metal from the reactivity series above that can be extracted using the same process as tin extraction.

....

[1]

[Total 2 marks]

2 A manufacturing company wants to extract a metal for use as a component in a car. After consideration, they decide to use either aluminium or iron.

Shona looks at the reactivity series below and makes the following statement:

Aluminium	Al	Most Reactive
Carbon	C	
Iron	Fe	Least Reactive

It will be cheaper to extract aluminium from its ore than iron.

Explain why Shona is wrong.

....

....

....

....

....

....

[Total 4 marks]

3 The increasing demand and the limited supply of metal-rich ores means that scientists are now developing new ways to extract metal from low-grade ores. *(Grade 6-7)*

a) Explain what phytoextraction is and how it is used to produce a substance containing copper compounds.

....

....

....

....

[5]

b) Describe **two** ways in which copper metal can be extracted from the product of phytoextraction.

....

....

[2]

c) Give **one** advantage and **one** disadvantage of using phytoextraction to extract metals from their ores.

....

....

....

[2]

d) Name one other biological method of extracting metals from low-grade ores.

....

[1]

[Total 10 marks]

4 Zinc is extracted from zinc oxide (ZnO) by heating it with carbon. *(Grade 7-9)*

a) Write a balanced equation for this reaction.

....

[2]

b) A certain batch of zinc oxide was heated with carbon. The zinc oxide contained impurities of iron oxide and calcium oxide. After the reaction was complete, any metal produced by the reaction was removed. Any unreacted metal oxides were left in the reaction vessel.

The zinc metal product was tested for purity and was found to contain traces of another metal. Suggest an identity for the other metal and explain why it was present.

....

....

....

....

[2]

[Total 4 marks]

Chapter C3 — Chemicals of the Natural Environment

Oxidation and Reduction

1 The combustion of hydrocarbons can be described as an oxidation reaction. Explain why. *(Grade 4-6)*

....

....

[Total 1 mark]

2 Place a tick (✓) in the box next to the **false** statement. *(Grade 4-6)*

Oxidation is the gain of oxygen. ☐

Reduction and oxidation happen at the same time. ☐

Reduction is the loss of electrons. ☐

When a metal reacts with oxygen to form a metal oxide, the metal is oxidised. ☐

[Total 1 mark]

3 In a redox reaction, aluminium atoms are oxidised to Al^{3+} ions. *(Grade 6-7)*

a) Write a balanced half equation to show this reaction. Use e^- to represent an electron.

....

[1]

b) The other half equation in this reaction is: $Cu^{2+} + 2e^- \rightarrow Cu$
Write a balanced ionic equation for the reaction that takes place.

....

[1]

[Total 2 marks]

4 The following ionic equation shows a redox reaction involving hydrogen ions and zinc. *(Grade 7-9)*

$$Zn + 2H^+ \rightarrow Zn^{2+} + H_2$$

a) Write balanced half equations to show how electrons are transferred in this reaction.
Use e^- to represent an electron.

i) Zinc half equation: ....

[1]

ii) Hydrogen half equation: ....

[1]

b) Which element was oxidised in the reaction?

....

[1]

[Total 3 marks]

Electrolysis

Fill in the labels on the diagram, using the words below,
to show the different parts of the electrochemical cell.

wires   cathode   electrolyte   power supply   anode

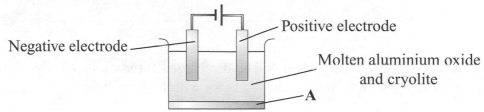

1   As part of an industrial process, a sample of sodium chloride, NaCl, was electrolysed.

a) Before the sodium chloride is electrolysed, it either has to be molten or dissolved in solution.
    Explain why this is necessary.

    ....

    ....
    [2]

b) Given that inert electrodes were used and the sodium chloride was molten,
    describe the movements of the ions in the electrolyte during electrolysis.

    ....

    ....
    [1]

    [Total 3 marks]

2   The diagram below shows a model of the process used in the
     industrial extraction of aluminium. Aluminium oxide is melted
     and electrolysed. Metallic aluminium is made at the cathode.

Negative electrode —   Positive electrode

                                Molten aluminium oxide
                                   and cryolite

                          A

a) What is the liquid labelled **A**?

    ....
    [1]

b) Why does the anode need to be replaced regularly?

    ....

    ....
    [2]

    [Total 3 marks]

Chapter C3 — Chemicals of the Natural Environment

3 Electrolysis is carried out on a solution of copper chloride, $CuCl_2$, using inert electrodes. (Grade 6-7)

a) Which of the following ions is **not** present in the solution?
Place a tick (✓) in the box next to the correct answer.

☐ H^+ ☐ H_2O^- ☐ Cl^- ☐ Cu^{2+}

[1]

b) What would you expect to see happen at:

i) the anode? ....

ii) the cathode? ....

[2]

[Total 3 marks]

4 The two half equations below show the reactions happening at the anode and the cathode during an electrolysis experiment. (Grade 6-7)

$$Pb^{2+} + 2e^- \rightarrow Pb$$
$$2I^- \rightarrow I_2 + 2e^-$$

a) Give the chemical formula of the electrolyte, given that it's a molten metal compound.

....

[1]

b) What would you expect to happen at the cathode?

....

[1]

[Total 2 marks]

5 Matthew carries out an electrolysis experiment using inert electrodes.
The electrolyte he uses is a solution of potassium nitrate. (Grade 6-7)

a) Explain what is meant, in this context, by the term 'inert'.

....

[1]

b) Matthew predicts that potassium will be discharged at the cathode. Given that potassium is more reactive than hydrogen, do you agree with Matthew? Explain your answer.

....

....

[2]

c) Describe what you would expect to see happening at the anode. Explain your answer.

....

....

[2]

[Total 5 marks]

Chapter C3 — Chemicals of the Natural Environment

6 A student investigated the products of electrolysis of a variety of aqueous solutions using inert electrodes.

a) Draw a labelled diagram of suitable apparatus that could be used for an experiment to collect gaseous products from the electrolysis of an aqueous solution.

[4]

b) Complete the table below by predicting the products at the anode and cathode for each of the solutions.

Solution	Product at cathode	Product at anode
$CuCl_2$		
KBr		
H_2SO_4		

[6]

c) When potassium nitrate solution is electrolysed neither potassium nor nitrogen are discharged. Explain why and state what is produced instead.

....

....

....
[4]

d) Write two half equations for the reaction that occurs when water is electrolysed.

Cathode: ....

Anode: ....

[2]

[Total 16 marks]

Exam Practice Tip

Electrolysis can be a hard subject to get your head around, and adding the electrolysis of aqueous solutions into the mix doesn't make it any easier. But remember, in aqueous solution, different ions can be discharged depending on their reactivity. Make sure you know the different ions that can be removed from solution, and in what situations that will happen — it really isn't too complicated once you know what you are doing, but you do need to learn the rules.

Covalent Bonding

1   The dot and cross diagrams of some simple covalent molecules are shown below. Draw out the displayed formulas of these molecules using straight lines to represent covalent bonds. One molecule (H_2) has been done as an example.

Dot and cross diagram   **Displayed formula**

H ⊗ H   H —— H

O
H + + H

H ⊗ Cl

[Total 2 marks]

2   This question is about the forces in simple molecular substances.

a)   Compare the strength of the bonds that hold the atoms in a molecule together with the forces that exist between different molecules.

....

....

[2]

b)   When a simple molecular substance melts, is it the bonds between atoms or the forces between molecules that are broken?

....

[1]

[Total 3 marks]

3   Iodine, I_2, is a simple molecular substance.

a)   At room temperature, iodine is a solid. Explain, with reference to the forces between molecules, why this is unusual for a simple molecular substance.

....

....

[2]

b)   Predict, with reasoning, whether iodine can conduct electricity in any state.

....

....

[2]

[Total 4 marks]

Chapter C3 — Chemicals of the Natural Environment

4 Methane is a covalent molecule. The structure of methane can be shown in a number of different ways. Two such diagrams are shown below.

$$H \overset{\bullet\times}{\underset{\bullet\times}{C}} H$$

with H above and H below

H—C—H with H above and H below

a) Suggest **two** ways of telling from the diagrams that methane is a covalent molecule.

....

....

[2]

b) State **two** ways in which the diagrams do **not** represent a methane molecule accurately.

....

....

[2]

c) Briefly describe how the hydrogen atoms in a methane molecule are bonded to the carbon atom.

....

....

....

[3]

[Total 7 marks]

5 Both methane (CH_4) and butane (C_4H_{10}) are simple covalent compounds that are gases at room temperature. Methane has a lower boiling point than butane.

a) Explain, in terms of particles, what happens when methane boils and why the boiling point of methane is lower than that of butane.

....

....

....

....

....

....

[5]

b) Explain why a carbon atom can form up to four covalent bonds, whilst a hydrogen atom only ever forms one covalent bond.

....

....

....

[2]

[Total 7 marks]

Chapter C3 — Chemicals of the Natural Environment

Empirical Formulas

1   The compound butane-1,4-diamine has the molecular formula $C_4H_{12}N_2$.   *(Grade 4-6)*
Which of the following is the empirical formula of butane-1,4-diamine?

Place a tick (✓) in the box next to the correct answer.

C_2H_5N ☐ $C_2H_6N_2$ ☐

CH_3N ☐ C_2H_6N ☐

[Total 1 mark]

2   Compound R has the empirical formula $C_6H_5O_2$.   *(Grade 6-7)*
Each molecule of compound R contains 10 hydrogen atoms.

What is the molecular formula of compound R?

....
[Total 2 marks]

3   Oct-1-ene is a compound with the molecular formula C_8H_{16}.   *(Grade 6-7)*
Emmy says the empirical formula of oct-1-ene is C_2H_4.

Is Emmy correct? Explain your answer.

....

....

....
[Total 1 mark]

4   Compound Q has the empirical formula C_2HF.   *(Grade 7-9)*
The relative formula mass of compound Q is 132.0.

What is the molecular formula of compound Q?

....
[Total 3 marks]

Chapter C3 — Chemicals of the Natural Environment   ☹ ☐   ☺ ☐   ☺ ☐

Homologous Series and Alkanes

Warm-Up

Place each of the compounds on the left below in the correct column of the table depending on whether or not they are hydrocarbons.

propane
ethene
lithium hydroxide
C_2H_6
CH_3CH_2Cl
C_2H_4
hydrochloric acid

Hydrocarbon	Not a hydrocarbon

1 The molecular formulas for five hydrocarbons, **A** to **E**, are shown below. Grade 4-6

A C_4H_8 **B** C_4H_{10} **C** C_5H_{10} **D** C_5H_{12} **E** C_6H_{14}

a) What is a hydrocarbon?

....

[1]

b) i) Which of the hydrocarbons, **A-E**, is butane?

....

[1]

ii) Draw the displayed formula of butane.

[1]

c) Which of the hydrocarbons are alkanes? Explain your answer.

....

....

[2]

d) Which of the hydrocarbons is likely to have the highest boiling point? Explain your answer.

....

....

[2]

[Total 7 marks]

2 The hydrocarbons in crude oil belong to several different homologous series. Compounds in a homologous series all share the same general formula. Give **three** other characteristics of the compounds in a homologous series.

Grade 6-7

....

....

....

....

....

[Total 3 marks]

3 Petrol and diesel are both fuels containing mixtures of hydrocarbons. The average chain length of the hydrocarbons in petrol and diesel are different, which causes diesel to have a higher boiling point than petrol.

Grade 6-7

a) Compare the viscosity of petrol and diesel.
   Explain your answer with reference to the information above.

   ....

   ....

   [2]

b) Predict whether petrol or diesel will be more flammable.
   Explain your answer with reference to the information above.

   ....

   ....

   [2]

c) Diesel contains alkanes that have 20 carbon atoms.
   Give the molecular formula of an alkane with 20 carbon atoms.

   ....

   [1]

d) Petrol contains alkanes with 8 carbon atoms.
   Finish and balance the equation for the complete combustion of this hydrocarbon

   .... C_8H_{18} + ... O_2 → .... + ...

   [2]
   [Total 7 marks]

Exam Practice Tip

Homologous series of organic compounds all have similar trends in properties such as their boiling points, viscosity and flammability. So you only need to learn these trends once and then you'll be ready to apply them to any homologous series you might come across in the exams. It's like a bargain many-for-the-price-of-one revision offer. Sweet.

Chapter C3 — Chemicals of the Natural Environment

Fractional Distillation of Crude Oil

1   A student carries out an experiment to separate a crude oil substitute into different fractions. The student sets up the apparatus as shown in the diagram below.

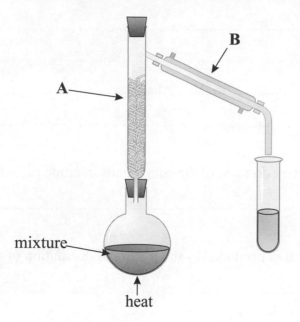

a) Name the pieces of equipment labelled **A** and **B**.

    i) **A**: ....
                                 [1]

    ii) **B**: ....
                                   [1]

b) State one way in which the equipment has been set up incorrectly,
    and explain how this could affect the results of the experiment.

    ....

    ....
                                     [2]

c) The student uses an electric heater to heat the mixture.
    Suggest **one** reason why the student chose not to use a Bunsen burner.

    ....

    ....
                                     [1]

d) The student changes the collection tube each time the temperature has risen by 50 °C until she
    has collected four fractions. Explain what is meant by the term 'fraction' in this context.

    ....

    ....
                                     [1]

[Total 6 marks]

2   Crude oil can be separated using the process of fractional distillation. The length of the hydrocarbon chains is fundamental to this process.

Grade
7-9

a)   Outline the industrial process of fractional distillation.

....

....

....

....

....

....

[4]

b)   What homologous series do most of the compounds in crude oil belong to?

....

[1]

c)   Name **one** fraction that is produced by the fractional distillation of crude oil.

....

[1]

d)   The table below shows the boiling points of some molecules that are present in fractions produced when crude oil is fractionated.

Hydrocarbon	Chemical formula	Boiling point (°C)
Heptane	C_7H_{16}	98
Triacontane	$C_{30}H_{62}$	450

i)   Which hydrocarbon would you expect to be collected **further down** the column?

....

[1]

ii) Explain your answer, with reference to the intermolecular bonding present between the hydrocarbons.

....

....

....

....

....

....

[4]

[Total 11 marks]

Chapter C3 — Chemicals of the Natural Environment

Uses of Crude Oil

1 Some hydrocarbons from crude oil are processed by the petrochemical industry.
For instance, decane, $C_{10}H_{22}$, can undergo cracking as shown in the following equation:
$$C_{10}H_{22} \rightarrow C_8H_{18} + C_2H_4$$

a) Explain why a petrochemical company may need to crack hydrocarbons.

....

....

[2]

b) Cracking can form a variety of products. Write an alternative balanced equation for the cracking
of decane.

....

[1]

[Total 3 marks]

2 Hydrocarbon fractions, produced by the fractional distillation of crude oil, are important
chemicals used in many industrial processes. The graph below shows the approximate
percentage of each fraction produced by an oil refinery, and the demand for each fraction.

a) The demand for diesel is greater than the supply.
Name **two** other fractions whose demand is greater than their supply.

....

[2]

b) Suggest what could be done to ensure that the supply of diesel matches the demand.

....

....

[1]

[Total 3 marks]

Exam Practice Tip

When balancing cracking equations, make sure that there's at least one alkane and one alkene in the products. Also, just like any chemical equation, remember to check that the numbers of each atom on both sides of the equation are the same.

    Chapter C3 — Chemicals of the Natural Environment

Alkenes

1   Alkanes and alkenes can take part in complete combustion reactions.

Which of the following shows the **correct** word equation for the complete combustion of ethene? Place a tick (✓) in the box next to the correct answer.

ethene + oxygen → carbon monoxide + water ☐

ethene + carbon dioxide → oxygen + water ☐

ethene + oxygen → carbon dioxide + water ☐

ethene + water → carbon dioxide + oxygen ☐

[Total 1 mark]

2   A student is investigating the chemical structure of alkenes.

a) Give the general formula for alkenes.

....

[1]

b) Place a tick (✓) in the box next to the displayed formula of ethene.

[1]

c) Methane is an alkane with one carbon atom. The student notices that there is not an alkene with only one carbon atom. Explain why an alkene with one carbon atom does **not** exist.

....

....

[1]

[Total 3 marks]

3 A student was investigating the reactivity of some hydrocarbons in the lab.

a) The student added a sample of a hydrocarbon, **A**, to bromine water and allowed it to react. The chemical formula of the product formed was $C_3H_6Br_2$. Draw the displayed formula of the original hydrocarbon, **A**.

[1]

b) What would the student see happen when the hydrocarbon, **A**, was added to the bromine water, and was then allowed to react?

....

[1]

c) In a separate experiment, bromine water was added to a sample of butene and a reaction occurred. Which of the following structures **could** have been formed by the reaction?

$$H-\underset{\underset{\displaystyle H}{|}}{\overset{\overset{\displaystyle H}{|}}{C}}-\underset{\underset{\displaystyle H}{|}}{\overset{\overset{\displaystyle H}{|}}{C}}-\underset{\underset{\displaystyle Br}{|}}{\overset{\overset{\displaystyle H}{|}}{C}}-\underset{\underset{\displaystyle Br}{|}}{\overset{\overset{\displaystyle H}{|}}{C}}-H \quad \square$$

$$H-\underset{\underset{\displaystyle H}{|}}{\overset{\overset{\displaystyle H}{|}}{C}}-\underset{\underset{\displaystyle H}{|}}{\overset{\overset{\displaystyle H}{|}}{C}}-\underset{\underset{\displaystyle Br}{|}}{\overset{\overset{\displaystyle Br}{|}}{C}}-\underset{\underset{\displaystyle H}{|}}{\overset{\overset{\displaystyle H}{|}}{C}}-H \quad \square$$

$$H-\underset{\underset{\displaystyle H}{|}}{\overset{\overset{\displaystyle H}{|}}{C}}-\underset{\underset{\displaystyle H}{|}}{\overset{\overset{\displaystyle H}{|}}{C}}-\underset{\underset{\displaystyle H}{|}}{\overset{\overset{\displaystyle Br}{|}}{C}}=C\overset{\displaystyle Br}{\underset{\displaystyle H}{}} \quad \square$$

$$H-\underset{\underset{\displaystyle Br}{|}}{\overset{\overset{\displaystyle H}{|}}{C}}-\underset{\underset{\displaystyle Br}{|}}{\overset{\overset{\displaystyle H}{|}}{C}}-\underset{\underset{\displaystyle H}{|}}{\overset{\overset{\displaystyle H}{|}}{C}}-\underset{\underset{\displaystyle H}{|}}{\overset{\overset{\displaystyle Br}{|}}{C}}-H \quad \square$$

[1]

[Total 3 marks]

4 Propene is a feedstock for the production of many useful organic compounds.

a) Interhalogen compounds such as ICl contain 2 different halogen atoms. They react with alkenes in a similar way to halogens. Draw the displayed formula of **one** of the two possible products that could form in a reaction between ICl and propene.

[1]

b) Propene also reacts with steam in the presence of a catalyst. There are two possible products of this reaction. Draw the displayed formulas of the two different products.

[2]

[Total 3 marks]

Alcohols and Carboxylic Acids

Identify which of the following functional groups represents alcohols. Tick **one** box.

C=C ☐   -COO⁻ ☐

-NO₂ ☐   -OH ☐

-COOH ☐   -NH₃ ☐

1 Alcohols are a series of organic compounds with a wide range of industrial applications. (Grade 4-6)

a) An alcohol containing three carbons is commonly used as a solvent.
What is the name given to this alcohol?

....
[1]

b) Ethanol is present in alcoholic drinks. Give the chemical formula for ethanol.

....
[1]

c) Which two products are formed when an alcohol is completely combusted?
Place a tick (✓) in the box next to the correct answer.

CO and H_2O ☐   CO and H_2 ☐

CO_2 and H_2O ☐ CO_2 and H_2 ☐

[1]

[Total 3 marks]

2 Under certain conditions, alcohols can be oxidised to form carboxylic acids. (Grade 4-6)

a) What is the functional group of a carboxylic acid?

....
[1]

b) Give the chemical formula for propanoic acid.

....
[1]

c) Name the carboxylic acid with the chemical formula CH_3COOH.

....
[1]

[Total 3 marks]

3 Methanol and butanol are both alcohols.

a) Draw the displayed formula of methanol.

[1]

b) Give one similarity and one difference between the structures of methanol and butanol.

....

....
[2]

c) Why do methanol and butanol both react in similar ways?

....
[1]

[Total 4 marks]

4 Two organic molecules, **Y** and **Z**, were added to separate test tubes and mixed with an excess of an oxidising agent. A reaction only took place in one of the test tubes.

a) The two possible organic molecules are shown below. Identify which molecule, **Y** or **Z**, reacted with the oxidising agent. Explain your answer.

Y

```
     H   H   H   H
     |   |   |   |
 H — C — C — C — C — O — H
     |   |   |   |
     H   H   H   H
```

Z

```
     H   H   H   H
     |   |   |   |
 H — C — C — C — C — H
     |   |   |   |
     H   H   H   H
```

....

....

....

....
[2]

b) Draw the displayed formula of the organic product formed when the oxidation reaction was complete.

[1]

[Total 3 marks]

Chapter C3 — Chemicals of the Natural Environment

Addition Polymers

1   Poly(ethene) is a polymer used in packaging applications.   (Grade 4-6)

a)   Name the monomer used to form poly(ethene).

....

[1]

b)   What type of polymerisation reaction occurs to form poly(ethene) from its monomer?

....

[1]

c)   What functional group is involved in the formation of poly(ethene) from its monomer?

....

[1]

[Total 3 marks]

2   The following question is about addition polymers.   (Grade 6-7)

a)   Place a tick (✓) in the box that shows the homologous series that can form addition polymers.

alkenes and alkanes   ☐   carboxylic acids only   ☐

alkenes only   ☐   alcohols and carboxylic acids   ☐

[1]

b)   The formula of vinyl acetate is shown to the right.
Vinyl acetate polymerises to form polyvinyl acetate.
Draw the displayed formula of polyvinyl acetate.

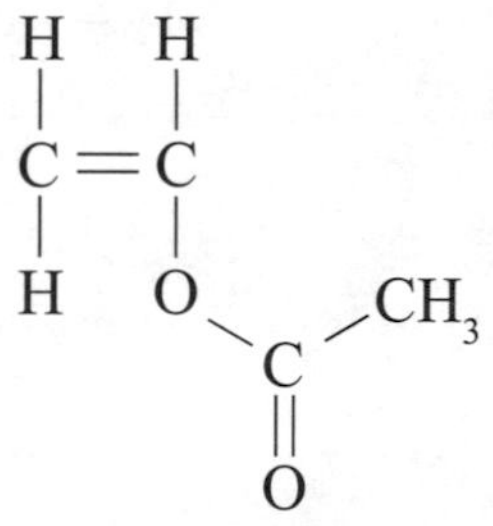

[1]

c)   The displayed formula of polypropene is shown
to the right. Draw the formula of its monomer.

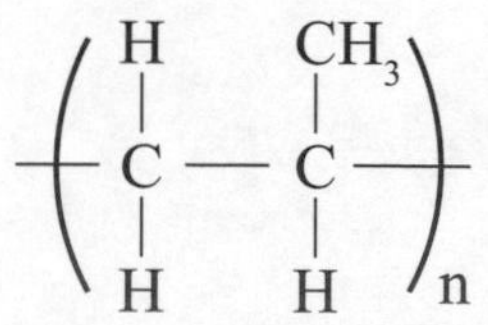

[1]

[Total 3 marks]

3 A class are carrying out an investigation to look at monomers and addition polymers. **Grade 6-7**

$$\begin{array}{cc} H & CH_3 \\ | & | \\ C & = C \\ | & | \\ H & C = O \\ & | \\ & O - CH_3 \end{array}$$

a) The students are shown the displayed formula of the monomer methyl methacrylate. This monomer is shown to the right. Selena believes that it can form an addition polymer but Jenna disagrees. State which student you agree with and why.

....

....

[1]

b) The students study poly(tetrafluoroethene), PTFE.
   A section of the polymer chain is shown below.

$$\begin{array}{cccccccc} F & F & F & F & F & F & F & F \\ | & | & | & | & | & | & | & | \\ -C-&C-&C-&C-&C-&C-&C-&C- \\ | & | & | & | & | & | & | & | \\ F & F & F & F & F & F & F & F \end{array}$$

Which of the monomers below forms the polymer, poly(tetrafluoroethene)?
Place a tick (✓) in the box next to the correct answer.

$$\begin{array}{cc} F & F \\ | & | \\ H-C-&C-H \\ | & | \\ F & F \end{array}$$ ☐

$$\begin{array}{cc} F & F \\ \diagdown & \diagup \\ C=&C \\ \diagup & \diagdown \\ F & F \end{array}$$ ☐

$$\begin{array}{cc} F & F \\ \diagdown & \diagup \\ C=&C \\ \diagup & \diagdown \\ H & H \end{array}$$ ☐

$$\begin{array}{cc} F & F \\ | & | \\ H-C-&C-H \\ | & | \\ H & H \end{array}$$ ☐

[1]

c) i) The class are discussing how addition polymers are formed synthetically. John says that you just need to mix the monomers together. Chris says that further conditions are generally required. Suggest **two** conditions that are often needed for addition polymerisation.

....

[1]

ii) Describe how new bonds form between the monomers during addition polymerisation.

....

....

[1]

[Total 4 marks]

Exam Practice Tip

If you're asked to find the monomer from an addition polymer chain, you'll first need to find the repeating unit. The carbon backbone in the repeating unit only has two C atoms. So start by drawing these two C atoms and put a double bond between them. Then look at the polymer chain to work out what groups surround them. Draw the groups in and voilà.

Chapter C4 — Material Choices

Condensation Polymers

1   Condensation polymerisation is used to produce many different polymers.   Grade 4-6

a)   Which of the following is **true** about condensation polymerisation?
Place a tick (✓) in the box next to the correct answer.

The monomers have carbon-carbon double bonds.   ☐

The repeating unit of the polymer has the same atoms as the combined monomers.   ☐

A small molecule is lost when condensation polymers are formed.   ☐

A small molecule is gained when condensation polymers are formed.   ☐

[1]

b)   How many functional groups does each monomer need to have to undergo condensation polymerisation?

....

[1]

[Total 2 marks]

2   Ethane-1,2-diol and hexanedioic acid polymerise to produce a polyester, **D**.   Grade 6-7
The reactants are shown in the diagram below.

$$n \; HO-\underset{\underset{H}{|}}{\overset{\overset{H}{|}}{C}}-\underset{\underset{H}{|}}{\overset{\overset{H}{|}}{C}}-OH \; + \; n \; \underset{HO}{\overset{O}{\diagdown}}C-(CH_2)_4-C\underset{OH}{\overset{O}{\diagup}} \longrightarrow D \; + \; 2n \; E$$

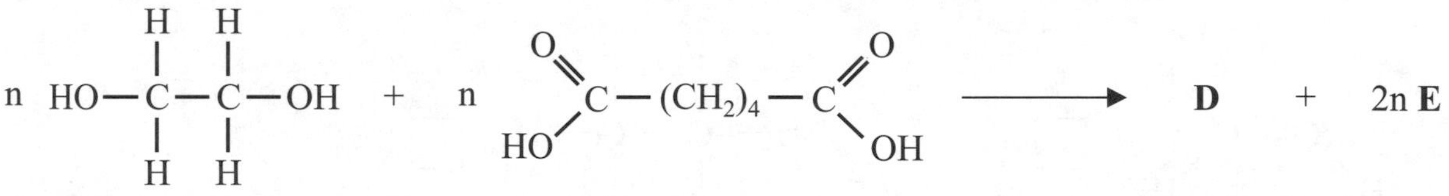

a)   What is the formula of **E**?

....

[1]

b)   Draw the displayed formula of polyester **D**.

[2]

c)   Would it be possible to form a polymer from just one of the
monomer reactants in the diagram? Explain your answer.

....

....

[1]

[Total 4 marks]

Chapter C4 — Material Choices

3 Some polymers are made by condensation polymerisation.

a) The structure of propylamine is shown below.
Is this molecule able to form condensation polymers or not? Explain your answer.

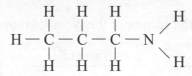

....

....

....

....
[2]

b) Nylon 6,6 is an example of a polyamide.
The displayed formula of nylon 6,6 is shown below.

$$\left[\begin{array}{c} \overset{O}{\underset{\parallel}{C}} - \overset{H}{\underset{H}{C}} - \overset{H}{\underset{H}{C}} - \overset{H}{\underset{H}{C}} - \overset{H}{\underset{H}{C}} - \overset{O}{\underset{\parallel}{C}} - \overset{}{N} - \overset{H}{\underset{H}{C}} - \overset{H}{\underset{H}{C}} - \overset{H}{\underset{H}{C}} - \overset{H}{\underset{H}{C}} - \overset{H}{\underset{H}{C}} - \overset{H}{\underset{H}{C}} - \overset{}{N} \end{array} \right]_n$$

Circle the amide link that has formed between the two monomers.
[1]

c) Water was released in the formation of nylon 6,6.
Draw the displayed formula for the two monomers.

[2]

d) Name the two types of monomer that form this condensation polymer.

....
[2]

[Total 7 marks]

Chapter C4 — Material Choices

More on Polymers

1 Some condensation polymers occur naturally and are essential to our growth and survival.

a) Complete the table below with the names of the types of monomer that form the polymers.

Polymer	Protein	Starch
Monomer	....	....

[2]

b) i) Name a naturally occurring polymer that is formed from nucleotide monomers.

....

[1]

ii) State how many different types of nucleotide make up this polymer.

....

[1]

[Total 4 marks]

2* Look at the information below. It describes some properties of two polymers, Y and Z.
Polymers Y and Z are not made from the same monomer.

Polymer Y
• contains carbon and hydrogen atoms only
• does not melt when heated
• rigid

Polymer Z
• contains carbon and hydrogen atoms only
• melts when heated
• flexible

Suggest and explain the reasons for the differences in the properties of the two polymers.
Give your answer in terms of the nature and arrangement of their chemical bonds.

....

....

....

....

....

....

....

....

....

....

[Total 6 marks]

Chapter C4 — Material Choices

Giant Covalent Structures

Circle the diagram below that represents a compound with a giant covalent structure.

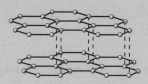 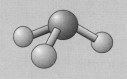 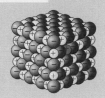

1 The diagrams below show two different types of carbon structure.

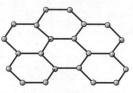

Structure A   **Structure B**

a) Name the two carbon structures shown.

Structure **A**: ....

Structure **B**: ....

[2]

b) One of the structures can be used to make components in electrical circuits. Identify the correct structure and explain how its bonding and structure make it suitable for this use.

....

....

....

[3]

c) Both structures have very high melting points. Explain what causes this property.

....

....

....

[2]

d) Name **one** other allotrope of carbon that has a giant covalent structure and describe its bonding and structure.

....

....

....

....

[5]

[Total 12 marks]

Bulk Properties of Materials

Match the bulk property with the type of bonding or structure that causes it.

Easily reshaped	Bonds break when particles move
High tensile strength	Particles move without bonds breaking
Brittle	Particles held firmly in place

1   The table below lists several compounds that contain fluorine.   Grade 6-7

Name of compound	Formula	Structure	Electrical Conductivity
sodium fluoride	NaF	ionic	yes, when molten / dissolved in water
fluoroethane	C_2H_5F	simple molecular	none
poly(fluoroethene)	$(C_2H_3F)_n$	polymer	none

Describe the type of bonding in sodium fluoride and explain how its structure allows
for electrical conductivity, unlike fluoroethane and poly(fluoroethene).

....

....

....

....

....

[Total 4 marks]

2   The element phosphorus exists in several different forms including white phosphorus and
black phosphorus. White phosphorus is made of molecules of four phosphorus atoms.
Black phosphorus has a giant covalent structure.   Grade 6-7

Despite being made from the same element, white and black phosphorus have very different melting
points. Predict which type of phosphorus has the highest melting point. Explain your answer.

....

....

....

....

....

....

[Total 3 marks]

Chapter C4 — Material Choices

Types of Materials and Their Uses

1 Materials can be categorised into several different types. (Grade 4-6)

a) Match each of the materials with the group of materials it belongs to.

Glass	Alloy
Polystyrene	Polymer
Brass	Composite
Fibreglass	Ceramic

[4]

b) Describe what composite materials are and explain what determines their properties.

....

....

[2]

[Total 6 marks]

2 An alloy is a mixture of a metal and at least one other element. (Grade 6-7)
The table below shows some data about the properties of various alloys.

Alloy	Carbon Composition (%)	Strength (MPa)	Density (g/cm³)
Stainless steel	0.08	205	7.88
Low carbon steel	0.1	245	7.60
High carbon steel	1.5	355	7.84
Aluminium alloy	0	117	2.71

a) Using data from the table, state the effect on strength of increasing the carbon content in steel.

....

[1]

b) A vice is used to hold an object in place while work is carried out on it.
The material a vice is made from needs to be strong and heavy to hold objects in place.
Using data from the table, suggest an alloy which would be suitable for this purpose.

....

[1]

c) Aluminium alloy has the lowest strength value of all the metals shown in the table and yet it is used to make many parts of commercial aircraft. Using the data in the table, explain why this is.

....

[1]

[Total 3 marks]

3 The table below shows the properties of several different materials.

Material	Density (g/cm³)	Strength (MPa)	Resistance to Corrosion	Cost
PVC	1.3	52	Good	Low
Carbon fibre	1.5	4100	Good	High
Copper	8.9	220	Poor	Medium
Steel	7.8	780	Poor (but can be easily protected)	Low
Lead	11.3	12	Good	Low

a) A sports company is deciding on the best material for making a professional hockey stick.
Which material from the table would be the **most** suitable?
Use the data from the table to explain your answer.

....

....

....

....

....

[4]

b) Determine which material from the table is the **most** suitable for building bridges.
Explain your answer using information from the table.

....

....

....

....

....

[4]

c) Determine which material from the table would be the **most** suitable material to make drainpipes.
Explain your answer using information from the table.

....

....

....

....

[4]

[Total 12 marks]

Exam Practice Tip

You may need to decide, out of a choice of materials, which one is the most suitable for making something. Although physical properties are important, don't forget to look at cost. For example, carbon fibre is very strong but also very expensive — if you need to use a lot of it, like for building bridges, it'll cost a lot and this can sometimes be a problem.

Chapter C4 — Material Choices

Corrosion

1 Martha and Joe both own bikes with iron bike chains. Martha leaves her bike outside and, after a week, discovers that the chain has started to rust. *(Grade 6-7)*

a) When iron rusts, there is an addition of oxygen to the iron atoms. What is this process called?

....

[1]

b) Joe keeps his bike in his house. Is his bike more or less likely to rust than Martha's? Explain your answer.

....

....

[2]

c) i) Martha buys a new iron bike chain. Place a tick (✓) in the box that shows the **best** method that she could use to prevent her new chain from rusting.

painting ☐   galvanisation ☐   oiling ☐   electroplating ☐

[1]

ii) Explain your answer.

....

....

[2]

iii) State **one** way that this barrier method will help to improve the life cycle assessment of the bike.

....

[1]

[Total 7 marks]

2 There are several methods that can be used to prevent the corrosion of metals and alloys. *(Grade 6-7)*

a) A ship manufacturer wants to prevent the corrosion of a steel ship using sacrificial protection. Describe what is meant by sacrificial protection and explain how it protects the ship.

....

....

....

....

[3]

b) A roofing company coats an iron roof with a layer of zinc to protect it from rusting. After a while, the zinc layer becomes scratched. Would you expect the iron roofing to begin to rust? Explain your answer.

....

....

[2]

[Total 5 marks]

Chapter C4 — Material Choices

3 Gwen is investigating how different conditions affect the corrosion of an iron nail.

Gwen sets up four test tubes, labelled **A**, **B**, **C** and **D**. The set-up of her experiment is shown below. She leaves the test tubes for five days.

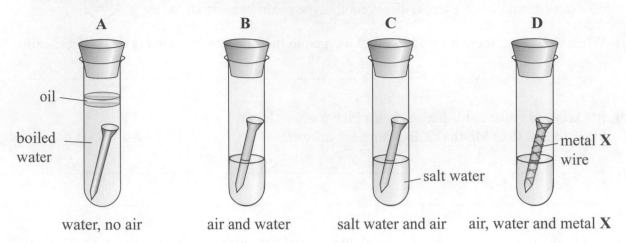

a) Gwen notices that the nail has rusted in test tube **B**, but the nail in test tube **A** is rust-free. Explain this difference.

....

....

[2]

b) Rusting also occurs in test tube **C**. The salt water in test tube **C** contains lots of dissociated ions which allow rapid transfer of electrons. Gwen observes that the nail in test tube **C** has rusted much more than the nail in test tube **B**. Suggest a reason for this difference in corrosion between the two conditions. Include details of the redox reaction that takes place during rusting.

....

....

....

....

....

....

[3]

c) A wire, made from metal **X**, is wrapped around the nail in test tube **D**. During the experiment, the nail does not rust. Gwen is told that metal **X** is either copper or magnesium. Using the reactivity series below, identify metal **X**. Explain your answer.

magnesium	most reactive
iron	↓
copper	least reactive

....

....

[2]

[Total 7 marks]

Reuse and Recycling

1 Rachel is sorting some rubbish that has accumulated around her house.

a) Rachel has three pieces of rubbish made from three different materials, **A**, **B** and **C**. Some data about the materials is shown in the table below.

Material	Availability of resource	Energy to recycle	Energy to extract
A	Abundant	High	Low
B	Limited	Low	High
C	Limited	Medium	High

From the data given, which material in the table is the **best** to recycle? Explain your answer.

....

....

....

....

[2]

b)* Rachel has some plastic bottles made from PET. She is able to recycle plastic bottles at her local recycling centre. Rachel's friend Mike says that he normally throws his PET bottles away with the waste that gets sent to landfill. Discuss why it is better to recycle PET bottles rather than send them to landfill.

....

....

....

....

....

....

....

....

[6]

c) Give **two** reasons why some materials may be made from scratch rather than from recycled material.

....

....

[2]

[Total 10 marks]

Life Cycle Assessments

1   A furniture company is designing a new chair for children.
They need to decide whether the chair will be made out of polypropene or timber.

Material	Source	Relative Energy Cost to Make/Extract	Recyclability
Timber	Trees	1	Recyclable
Polypropene	Crude oil	15	Recyclable

a)   The company carries out a life cycle assessment of both possible products.
Describe the purpose of a life cycle assessment.

....

....
[1]

b)   Using the data in the table above, explain which material would be the **best** choice
to make the chair from, in terms of sustainability. Explain your answer.

....

....

....

....

....
[3]

c)   Suggest **two** further factors, that aren't discussed in the table, that the company should consider in
their life cycle assessment, when deciding whether to make the chair from timber or polypropene.

....

....
[2]

[Total 6 marks]

2 A garden tool company is considering the environmental costs of producing a rake. **Grade 6-7**

a) The rake contains components made from iron.
Suggest **two** environmental problems associated with extracting iron from its ore.

....

....
[2]

b) The rake contains parts that cannot be recycled.
One option for disposal at the end of its lifespan is incineration.
Give **one** advantage and **one** disadvantage of incinerating waste as a means of disposal.

....

....
[2]

c) The rake is sold in plastic packaging. Suggest a way that consumers
could dispose of the packaging to reduce the environmental impact.

....
[1]

[Total 5 marks]

3 A toy company is carrying out a life cycle assessment of four prototype toys. **Grade 7-9**
The table below displays some of the data from their assessments.

Toy	CO_2 emissions (kg)	Solvent use (dm³)	Energy consumption (MJ)
A	16.2	3981	267.84
B	14.8	2672	212.26
C	14.9	3876	159.82
D	12.4	2112	174.56

Using the data in the table, evaluate the relative environmental impact of producing each toy.

....

....

....

....

....

....

....

[Total 4 marks]

Exam Practice Tip

You may be given data and asked to figure out which product has the biggest or smallest environmental impact. It's likely that there won't be an obvious answer at first glance — some products may have really low CO_2 emissions but may pollute lots of water. You'll have to look at _all_ the factors and decide which product is the best or worst overall.

Chapter C4 — Material Choices

Nanoparticles

1 Place a tick (✓) in the box next to the statement about nanoparticles which is **true**. (Grade 4-6)

Nanoparticles contain approximately one thousand atoms. ☐

Nanoparticles are 1-100 nm in size. ☐

All nanoparticles are the same size and shape. ☐

Nanoparticles are smaller than simple molecules, such as carbon dioxide. ☐

[Total 1 mark]

2 Nanoparticles of zinc oxide are used in some sunscreens to improve the protection of skin from exposure to sunlight. (Grade 4-6)

State **two** potential risks of using nanoparticles of zinc oxide in sunscreens.

....

....

[Total 2 marks]

3 The properties of some nanoparticles are listed in the table below. (Grade 6-7)

Nanoparticle	Properties
Carbon nanotubes	Forms a cage-like structure that can be used to trap small molecules. Light and strong.
Gold	Responds to touch, temperature and humidity. Changes colour in response to the concentration of other compounds in solution.
Silver	Antibacterial

Suggest, with reasoning, which material could be used for the following applications. You can use each material more than once, and you do not need to use every material.

a) Delivering drugs to specific parts of the body.

Material: ....

Reason: ....

[2]

b) Sterilising water in a water filter.

Material: ....

Reason: ....

[2]

c) Strengthening lightweight sports equipment, such as tennis racket strings.

Material: ....

Reason: ....

[2]

[Total 6 marks]

4 The surface area to volume ratio of an object can affect how it behaves. **Grade 6-7**

a) Calculate the volume of cube **A**, which has sides 10 nm long.

Volume = ... nm³
[1]

b) Calculate the total surface area of cube **A**.

Surface area = ... nm²
[2]

c) Use your answers to parts a) and b) to calculate the surface area to volume ratio of cube **A**.

Surface area to volume ratio = ...
[1]

d) Calculate the surface area to volume ratio of cube **B**, which has sides of 1 nm.

Surface area to volume ratio = ...
[4]

e) A quantity of cubes, each identical to cube **B**, were found to have a total volume of 500 nm³. Use your answer to part d) to calculate the total surface area of this quantity of cubes.

Surface area = ... nm²
[1]
[Total 9 marks]

5 Explain how the small size of nanoparticles gives them different properties from larger particles of the same material. **Grade 7-9**

....

....

....

....
[Total 3 marks]

Chapter C4 — Material Choices

Purity and Mixtures

1   Misty-Marie is doing a chemistry experiment.
The instructions say she needs to use pure water.
Stanley offers her a bottle labelled '100% Pure Spring Water'.

Grade 4-6

Suggest why Stanley's water is unlikely to be suitable for Misty-Marie's experiment.

....

....

....

....

[Total 2 marks]

2   A scientist is comparing two samples of the same compound.
One sample is pure, but the other contains a number of impurities.
The compound is a solid at room temperature.

Grade 4-6

The scientist decides to work out which is the pure sample by heating both samples
and recording their melting points. Explain how she will be able to tell which is the
pure sample, even if she does not know the melting point of the pure compound.

....

....

....

[Total 2 marks]

3   Gunpowder is a formulation of potassium nitrate, charcoal and sulfur in the ratio 15 : 3 : 2.

Grade 6-7

a)   What is meant by the term 'formulation'?

....

....

[1]

b)   Calculate the mass of charcoal in 40 g of gunpowder.

mass of charcoal = ... g

[3]

[Total 4 marks]

Chromatography

1   Olivia analysed an unknown mixture of liquids using paper chromatography. The solvent she used was ethanol. The chromatogram she produced is shown in the diagram below.

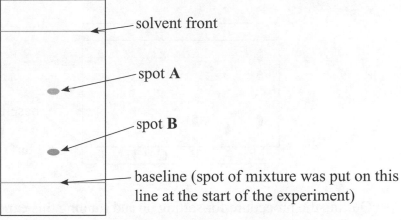

a)   Name the mobile phase in Olivia's experiment

....

[1]

b)   What does this chromatogram tell you about the number of components in the mixture?
Explain your answer.

....

....

[2]

c)   Calculate the Rf value of spot **B**. Use a ruler to help you.

$$Rf = \frac{\text{distance travelled by solute}}{\text{distance travelled by solvent}}$$

Rf = ...

[2]

d)   Olivia is given a list of five chemicals.
She is told that her mixture is made up of a combination of some of the chemicals on the list.
Explain how Olivia could use pure samples of the chemicals on the list
to identify the components of the mixture using paper chromatography.

....

....

....

....

[2]

[Total 7 marks]

2 Lamar wants to analyse the composition of a sample of ink.
The ink is made up of a number of dyes dissolved in a solvent.

a) Lamar uses paper chromatography to analyse the mixtures of dyes in the ink.
He compares the mixture with five different water-soluble dyes, A to E.
After 30 minutes, the chromatogram below was obtained.

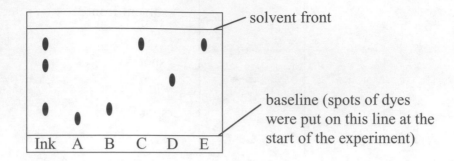

Outline the procedure for setting up and running this experiment.

....

....

....

....

....

....

....

[5]

b) Explain the results shown on Lamar's chromatogram.

....

....

....

....

....

....

[4]

c) All the dyes in Lamar's ink were coloured. Describe an additional step he would need
to add to his method if he were analysing a mixture of colourless compounds instead.

....

....

[1]

[Total 10 marks]

Chapter C5 — Chemical Analysis

Separating Mixtures

1* A student wants to separate the components of a mixture.
The mixture is a white powder composed of barium sulfate and potassium iodide.
The table below shows some information about the two compounds in the mixture.

Name	Melting point / °C	Boiling point / °C	Appearance at room temperature	Soluble in water?
barium sulfate	1580	1600	white solid	no
potassium iodide	681	1330	white solid	yes

Describe a detailed method that the student could use
to obtain pure samples of **both** compounds.

....

....

....

....

....

....

....

....

....

....

....

....

....

....

....

[Total 6 marks]

Chapter C5 — Chemical Analysis

2 Sodium chloride dissolves in water, but not in ethanol.
Sodium chloride has a melting point of 801 °C and a boiling point of 1413 °C.
Ethanol has a melting point of −114 °C and a boiling point of 78 °C.

a) Suggest a purification method which would separate a mixture of sodium chloride and ethanol, but **not** a mixture of sodium chloride and water. Explain your answer.

....

....

....

....
[3]

b) Suggest a purification method which would separate a mixture of sodium chloride and water and would **also** separate a mixture of sodium chloride and ethanol. Explain your answer.

....

....

....
[2]

[Total 5 marks]

3 The table below lists the boiling points of three compounds.

Name	Formula	Boiling point / °C
cyclopentane	C_5H_{10}	49
cyclohexane	C_6H_{12}	81
ethyl ethanoate	$C_4H_8O_2$	77

Suggest why a mixture of cyclohexane and ethyl ethanoate might be more difficult to separate than a mixture of cyclohexane and cyclopentane.

....

....

....

....

....

[Total 2 marks]

Exam Practice Tip

You might find some of these separation techniques cropping up in questions about other practicals — you often need to use one of them at the end of an experiment to separate out a pure sample of the product from the reaction mixture.

Tests for Ions

1 Kelly has a small bottle of a clear solution labelled "calcium sulfate solution". Her teacher asks her to perform some tests to confirm that the bottle of solution has been correctly labelled.

a) First Kelly tests the solution for calcium ions using the method shown in the box below. The name of the solution she used in step 1 has been replaced with 'Solution **A**'.

> Method for testing for calcium ions
> 1. Clean a nichrome wire loop by dipping it into Solution A, then holding it in a blue Bunsen flame.
> 2. Dip the wire loop into the test solution.
> 3. Put the wire loop in the clear part of a Bunsen flame.
> 4. Record the colour of the flame with the wire loop in it.

i) Suggest what Solution **A** is.

....

[1]

ii) State the colour of the flame that will be produced if the solution being tested does contain calcium ions.

....

[1]

b) Next, Kelly tests the solution for sulfate ions using the method shown in the box below. The name of the chemical she used in step 3 has been replaced with 'Reagent **X**'.

> Method for testing for sulfate ions
> 1. Place 3 cm^3 of your test solution in a test tube.
> 2. Add 3 cm^3 of hydrochloric acid.
> 3. Add 10 drops of Reagent **X** to the test tube and observe what happens.

Kelly's test solution does contain sulfate ions.
When she adds Reagent **X** to the test solution in step 3, a precipitate forms.

i) Suggest what Reagent **X** is.

....

[1]

ii) State the colour of the precipitate that forms when Reagent **X** is added in step 3.

....

[1]

[Total 4 marks]

Chapter C5 — Chemical Analysis

2 Various tests can be used to identify which metal ion is present in a compound. (Grade 4-6)

a) Suggest what metal ion is present in a compound that turns the flame crimson in a flame test.

....

[1]

b) Copper(II) nitrate is a soluble salt that contains Cu^{2+} ions.

   i) What colour would you expect this compound to produce in a flame test?

....

[1]

   ii) If you dissolved this compound in water and then added a few drops of sodium hydroxide solution, what would you expect to observe?

....

[1]

[Total 3 marks]

3 Mark is given samples of three solutions, **A**, **B**, and **C**. He tests each of them with acidified silver nitrate solution and sodium hydroxide solution. His table of results is shown below. (Grade 6-7)

Test	Solution A	Solution B	Solution C
Add acidified silver nitrate solution	yellow precipitate forms	no reaction	yellow precipitate forms
Add a few drops of sodium hydroxide solution	white precipitate forms	brown precipitate forms	green precipitate forms

a) Suggest which metal ion solution **B** contains.

....

[1]

b) Suggest the formula of the compound in solution **C**.

....

[1]

c) i) Mark says "I can tell from my results that solution **A** contains zinc ions." Explain why Mark is wrong.

....

....

[1]

   ii) If solution **A** did contain zinc ions, what would you expect Mark to observe if he added more sodium hydroxide solution to the test tube?

....

[1]

[Total 4 marks]

Chapter C5 — Chemical Analysis

4 The compound potassium sodium carbonate has the formula $KNaCO_3$. (Grade 6-7)

a) Explain why it would be difficult to identify the positive ions in this compound using a flame test.

....

....

[1]

b) Describe how you could test a solution of this compound to show that it contained carbonate ions. You should include details of a positive result.

....

....

....

....

[3]

[Total 4 marks]

5* Oliver was asked to prepare a sample of potassium chloride. He designed a suitable method and carried it out. When he had finished, he had 5 g of the solid salt. Describe how Oliver could show that the salt he has made is potassium chloride. In your answer you should give the methods for any tests that you suggest. (Grade 7-9)

....

....

....

....

....

....

....

....

....

....

....

....

....

[Total 6 marks]

Exam Practice Tip

The examiner might ask you to identify a salt in solution by looking at the results of different tests. Remember, a salt will contain both an anion and a cation, so if your answer only has ions with the <u>same</u> charge, you've probably made a mistake.

Chapter C5 — Chemical Analysis

Flame Emission Spectroscopy

1 Flame emission spectroscopy is an example of an instrumental method that can be used to analyse elements and compounds. **Grade 6-7**

a) State **two** advantages of using instrumental methods compared to chemical tests.

....

....

[2]

b) Lithium ions and strontium ions produce very similar-coloured flames in flame tests. Explain why it would be easier to distinguish between these two ions using flame emission spectroscopy.

....

....

[1]

c) Suggest **one** other way in which flame emission spectroscopy is more useful than flame tests for identifying metal ions in a substance.

....

....

[1]

[Total 4 marks]

2 Flame emission spectroscopy can be used to detect various positive ions within a mixture. The diagram below shows the spectra for Metal **A**, Metal **B**, Metal **C** and a mixture, **M**. **Grade 7-9**

Metal **A**

Metal **B**

Metal **C**

M

750   700   650   600   550   500   450   400
Wavelength (nm)

a) Describe how flame emission spectroscopy works.

....

....

....

[2]

b) Which metal ion(s) are in the mixture, **M**?

....

[1]

[Total 3 marks]

Relative Mass

Match up the following formulas with the correct relative formula mass of the substance.
Use the periodic table to help you.

F_2	38.0
C_2H_6	40.0
CaO	30.0
NaOH	56.1

1 The formula of the compound zinc cyanide is $Zn(CN)_2$.

Find the relative formula mass of zinc cyanide.

relative formula mass = ...

[Total 2 marks]

2 Magnesium oxide is a salt with the formula MgO.

a) Calculate the percentage mass of magnesium ions in magnesium oxide.

Percentage by mass of magnesium = ... %

[2]

b) A chemist is making a mixture that needs to contain 15% magnesium ions by mass.
Calculate the mass of magnesium in 200 g of this mixture.

Mass of magnesium = ... g

[1]

[Total 3 marks]

Chapter C5 — Chemical Analysis

80

Conservation of Mass

1 A student mixes 3.0 g of silver nitrate solution and 15.8 g of sodium chloride solution together in a flask. The following precipitation reaction occurs:

$$AgNO_{3\,(aq)} + NaCl_{(aq)} \rightarrow AgCl_{(s)} + NaNO_{3\,(aq)}$$

Predict the total mass of the contents of the flask after the reaction. Explain your answer.

....

....

....

[Total 2 marks]

2 A student is investigating a reaction between zinc and hydrochloric acid. The reaction produces hydrogen gas and a solution of zinc chloride. The student's experimental set-up is shown in the diagram below.

Conical flask

Hydrochloric acid

Zinc

Mass balance

124.568 g

a) How would you expect the mass of the conical flask and its contents to change over the course of the reaction? Explain your answer.

....

....

....

[2]

b) The student repeats the reaction, but this time attaches a gas syringe to the top of the flask. How would you expect the mass of the apparatus and its contents to change over the course of the reaction? Explain your answer.

....

....

....

....

[2]

[Total 4 marks]

Chapter C5 — Chemical Analysis

The Mole

1   What is the approximate number of atoms in 1 mole of carbon atoms? [Grade 4-6]

Place a tick (✓) in the box next to the correct answer.

7.2×10^{23} atoms   ☐

7.2×10^{24} atoms   ☐

6.0×10^{-23} atoms   ☐

6.0×10^{23} atoms   ☐

[Total 1 mark]

2   A pharmacist is synthesising aspirin, $C_9H_8O_4$, as part of a drugs trial. [Grade 4-6]
After the experiment, the pharmacist calculates that she has made 12.5 moles of aspirin.
What mass of aspirin has she made?

.... g

[Total 2 marks]

3   How many atoms are there in 7 moles of ammonia, NH_3? [Grade 6-7]
Give your answer to 3 significant figures.

.... atoms

[Total 2 marks]

4   The table below contains information about various atoms. Complete the table. [Grade 6-7]
Where appropriate, give any answers to 2 significant figures and in standard form.

Element	Atomic Number	Mass Number	Mass of 1 atom (g)
Hydrogen	1	1	....
Nitrogen	7	....	2.3×10^{-23}
Aluminium	13	27	....
Argon	....	40	6.7×10^{-23}
Titanium	22	48	....

[Total 5 marks]

Chapter C5 — Chemical Analysis

5 A sample of an unknown element contains 1.2×10^{25} atoms.

a) How many moles of atoms of the element are in the sample?

....

[1]

b) Given that the atoms have a mean mass of 9.3×10^{-23} g, what is the identity of the element?

....

[2]

[Total 3 marks]

6 A student is investigating an unidentified acid, which is made up of oxygen, sulfur and hydrogen atoms.

a) Given that 3.5 moles of the acid has a mass of 343.35 g, what is the relative formula mass of the acid?

....

[1]

b) The percentage mass of the acid made up of oxygen atoms is 65%.
To the nearest whole number, how many moles of oxygen atoms are in one mole of the acid?

....

[2]

c) In one mole of the acid, there is one mole of sulfur atoms.

i) Find the number of moles of hydrogen atoms in one mole of the acid.

....

[2]

ii) Use your answers to part b) and part c) i) to deduce the chemical formula of the acid.

....

[1]

[Total 6 marks]

Calculations Using Balanced Equations

Complete the following sentences by filling in the blanks with the words on the right.

1) If the amount of the limiting reactant in a reaction is decreased,
   then the amount of product made will ....

2) If the amount of the limiting reactant in a reaction is increased,
   then the amount of product made will ....

3) If the amount of an excess reactant is increased,
   then the amount of product made will ....

not change

decrease

increase

1 James is investigating the reactivity of some metals. As part of his investigation, he places a piece of magnesium metal in a flask containing an excess of hydrochloric acid and monitors the reaction. The reaction produces hydrogen gas and a metal salt solution.

Grade 4-6

a) Which of the reactants is the limiting reactant?

   ....

   [1]

b) James repeats the experiment but changes the starting quantities of magnesium and acid. He lets the reaction proceed to completion, and notes that once the reaction has finished, the reaction vessel contains a small amount of grey metal and a colourless solution.

   In this second experiment, which of the reactants is the limiting reactant? Explain your answer.

   ....

   ....

   ....

   [2]

   [Total 3 marks]

2 An industrial process converts the alkene ethene into ethanol, according to the reaction below.

Grade 6-7

$$C_2H_4 + H_2O \rightarrow CH_3CH_2OH$$

What mass of ethanol can be made from 53.2 g of ethene, given that water is in excess?

.... g

[Total 3 marks]

3 The following equation shows the complete combustion of ethane in air.

$$2C_2H_6 + 7O_2 \rightarrow 4CO_2 + 6H_2O$$

a) Given that 128 g of oxygen was burnt in the reaction, what mass of water was produced? Give your answer to three significant figures.

.... g

[3]

b) A company burns ethane to generate power for an industrial process.

As part of a carbon-reducing scheme, the company can only produce a maximum 4.4 tonnes of carbon dioxide per day (where 1 tonne = 1 000 000 g). What is the maximum amount of ethane that the company can burn each day so as not to exceed the limit of carbon dioxide?

.... tonnes

[3]

[Total 6 marks]

4 Urea, $(NH_2)_2CO$, is a compound that can be synthesised industrially using the following reaction.

$$2NH_3 + CO_2 \rightarrow (NH_2)_2CO + H_2O$$

a) A company makes 120.6 tonnes of urea each day (where 1 tonne = 1 000 000 g). What mass of carbon dioxide is required to make this mass?

.... tonnes

[3]

b) Usually the reaction happens in an excess of ammonia. However, a leak in the reaction vessel means the mass of ammonia entering the reaction chamber each day is reduced to 59.5 tonnes.

What is the decrease, in tonnes, in the amount of urea produced per day?

.... tonnes

[4]

[Total 7 marks]

Chapter C5 — Chemical Analysis

Calculations Using Moles

1 An unknown hydrocarbon, **A**, completely combusts in oxygen to produce just water and carbon dioxide.

   a) Given that four moles of carbon dioxide and four moles of water are produced during the combustion of 1 mole of **A**, suggest the chemical formula of hydrocarbon **A**.

....
[2]

   b) Write a balanced chemical equation for the complete combustion of **A**.

....
[1]

[Total 3 marks]

2 Viola reacts an element, **X**, with oxygen. The result of the reaction is a single product, an oxide of element **X**.

   a) Given that 200 g of **X** burns to produce 280 g of X oxide, what mass of oxygen gas was used in the reaction?

.... g
[1]

   b) Given that the relative atomic mass of **X** is 40, write a balanced equation for the reaction of **X** with oxygen in the air. You should represent **X** oxide as X_aO_b, where a and b are integers.

....
[4]

[Total 5 marks]

Chapter C5 — Chemical Analysis

3 A student reacts an unknown acid, H_2X, with sodium hydroxide, NaOH.
The products are a salt and water: $H_2X + 2NaOH \rightarrow Na_2X + 2H_2O$

a) The total mass of the reactants was 228.2 g, and 156.2 g of the salt was produced.
Calculate the number of moles of water produced.

.... moles
[2]

b) What mass of sodium hydroxide was used during this reaction?

.... g
[2]

c) Find the relative molecular mass of the unknown acid.

....
[3]
[Total 7 marks]

4 A scientist gently heats tin and iodine together. They react to form a single
product, which is a metal halide. Given that 3.57 g of tin reacts with
exactly 15.24 g of iodine, write a balanced equation for this reaction.

....
[Total 5 marks]

Exam Practice Tip

If a question involves dealing with moles of unknown masses, you can bet your bottom dollar that you're
going to need to be able to use the equations that link moles, mass and relative formula/atomic masses with
ease. Writing out this formula triangle that links these variables before you start these sorts of calculation
questions is always a good idea — it will help you to see what you can work out from what you're given.

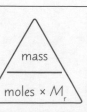

Percentage Yield

1 Kezia and Steven are reacting some lithium with water to form lithium hydroxide and hydrogen gas. From the mass of reactants, they calculate the theoretical yield of lithium hydroxide to be 25 g.

Grade 4-6

a) Kezia finds that 17 g of lithium hydroxide is produced.
What is the percentage yield of lithium hydroxide?
Place a tick (✓) in the box next to the correct answer.

63% ☐

72% ☐

68% ☐

54% ☐

[1]

b) Steven's experiment produces 22 g of lithium hydroxide.
Calculate the percentage yield of lithium hydroxide in his reaction.

Percentage yield = ... %

[2]

[Total 3 marks]

2 In a precipitation reaction, copper sulfate solution reacts with sodium hydroxide solution. The equation for the reaction is:
$$CuSO_4 + 2NaOH \rightarrow Cu(OH)_2 + Na_2SO_4$$

Grade 6-7

a) If 39.75 g of copper sulfate reacts with an excess of sodium hydroxide, calculate the theoretical yield of the copper hydroxide. Give your answer to 3 significant figures.

Theoretical yield = ... g

[3]

b) A student carries out this reaction and produces 16.5 g of copper hydroxide. Use your answer in part a) to calculate the percentage yield of the reaction to 3 significant figures.

Percentage yield = ... %

[2]

[Total 5 marks]

Chapter C5 — Chemical Analysis

3   When heated, calcium carbonate decomposes to form calcium oxide and carbon dioxide.
The equation for the reaction is: $CaCO_3 \rightarrow CaO + CO_2$

In an industrial reaction, 68.00 kg of calcium carbonate decomposed to form
28.56 kg of calcium oxide, CaO. Calculate the percentage yield of calcium oxide.

Percentage yield = ... %

[Total 5 marks]

4   Ammonia is produced in the Haber process by reacting nitrogen gas with hydrogen gas.
The equation for this reaction is: $N_2 + 3H_2 \rightleftharpoons 2NH_3$

a)   A factory used 14 kg of nitrogen gas to produce 4.5 kg of ammonia.
Calculate the percentage yield for the reaction.

Percentage yield = ... %

[5]

b)   Suggest **two** reasons why the percentage yield was less than 100%.

....

....

[2]

c)   Suggest **one** reason why it is desirable for a factory to obtain as high a percentage yield as possible.

....

....

[1]

[Total 8 marks]

Exam Practice Tip

Don't forget that percentage yield is just one factor that businesses consider when they're choosing a process to make chemicals in industry. Other factors they might need to consider include atom economy, rate of reaction and sustainability — these are all covered in Chapter C6.

Calculations with Gases

For the questions on this page, you may need the following information:
One mole of any gas occupies 24 dm³ at room temperature and pressure.

1 Hydrogen, H₂, and sulfur dioxide, SO₂, are both gases at room temperature and pressure.

a) Calculate the volume of 23.0 moles of H₂ at room temperature and pressure.

Volume = ... dm³
[1]

b) Calculate the volume of 96.15 g of SO₂ at room temperature and pressure.
(Relative formula mass of SO₂ = 64.1)

Volume = ... dm³
[2]

[Total 3 marks]

2 Carbon dioxide can be produced by reacting oxygen with carbon monoxide.
$$2CO_{(g)} + O_{2(g)} \rightarrow 2CO_{2(g)}$$

a) A student reacted 28.0 g of carbon monoxide with oxygen at room temperature and pressure.
Calculate the volume of oxygen involved in the reaction.

Volume of oxygen = ... dm³
[4]

b) Calculate the volume of carbon dioxide produced in the reaction in part a).

Volume of carbon dioxide = ... dm³
[1]

[Total 5 marks]

Chapter C5 — Chemical Analysis

Concentrations

Warm-Up

Three beakers of copper sulfate solution are shown below.
Circle the one that contains the **greatest mass** of copper sulfate.

Volume = 0.3 dm³
Concentration = 20 g/dm³

Volume = 0.1 dm³
Concentration = 45 g/dm³

Volume = 0.2 dm³
Concentration = 35 g/dm³

1 A student makes a saline solution by dissolving 36 g of sodium chloride in 0.40 dm³ of water. What is the concentration of the solution?

Place a tick (✓) in the box next to the correct answer.

90 g/dm³ ☐   14.4 g/dm³ ☐   14 400 g/dm³ ☐   0.090 g/dm³ ☐

[Total 1 mark]

2 28 g of calcium chloride was dissolved in 400 cm³ of water.

a) Calculate the concentration of the solution in g/dm³.

Concentration = ... g/dm³
[2]

b) Explain the term 'concentration of a solution'.

....

....
[1]
[Total 3 marks]

3 A solution of lithium hydroxide, LiOH, was made by dissolving 4.78 g of solid lithium hydroxide in 250 cm³ of water.

Calculate the concentration of the solution in mol/dm³.

Concentration = ... mol/dm³
[Total 3 marks]

Acids, Alkalis and Standard Solutions

1 Which of the following equations shows a neutralisation reaction? *Grade 4-6*

Place a tick (✓) in the box next to the correct answer.

$HNO_3 + LiOH \rightarrow LiNO_3 + H_2O$ ☐

$Mg + H_2O \rightarrow MgO + H_2$ ☐

$Na_2O + H_2O \rightarrow 2NaOH$ ☐

$C_4H_{10} + 6\frac{1}{2}O_2 \rightarrow 4CO_2 + 5H_2O$ ☐

[Total 1 mark]

2 Acids and bases react together in neutralisation reactions. *Grade 4-6*

a) Write the general word equation for a neutralisation reaction between an acid and a base.

....

[1]

b) Write an ionic equation, using hydrogen ions and hydroxide ions,
for a neutralisation reaction in aqueous solution.

....

[1]

[Total 2 marks]

3 Solution **X** is a standard solution of copper sulfate with a concentration of 75.0 g/dm³.
A student made up a volume of **X** by dissolving copper sulfate in 220 cm³ of water. *Grade 6-7*

a) Calculate the mass of copper sulfate that was used to make the solution.

Mass = ... g

[1]

b) Which of the following statements is **true**? Place a tick (✓) in the box next to the correct answer.

X will become more concentrated if more water is added to the solution. ☐

Dissolving 56 g of copper sulfate in 220 cm³ of water
will make a solution more concentrated than **X**. ☐

Adding an additional 10 g of the solute to **X** will make the solution less concentrated. ☐

The concentration of **X** will halve if an additional 10 cm³ of water is added to the solution. ☐

[1]

[Total 2 marks]

Chapter C5 — Chemical Analysis

4 A lab technician is making up some solutions for students to use in some of their classes. *(Grade 6-7)*

The technician makes a standard solution of sodium hydroxide for a titration experiment. She makes 600 cm³ of the solution at a concentration of 52 g/dm³.

a) Calculate the mass of sodium hydroxide in 600 cm³ of 52 g/dm³ sodium hydroxide solution.

mass = ... g

[2]

b) The technician weighs out the required mass of solid sodium hydroxide into a weighing container on a mass balance. She then transfers the sodium hydroxide into a beaker of deionised water.

i) Suggest **one** way in which she could make sure all the solid has been transferred to the beaker.

....

....

[1]

ii) Why is it important to use deionised water to make up the solution?

....

....

[1]

[Total 4 marks]

5 A student made a solution of sodium carbonate (Na_2CO_3) at a concentration of 0.50 mol/dm³. *(Grade 7-9)*

a) Calculate the number of moles of sodium carbonate in 0.50 dm³ of the solution.

.... mol

[1]

b) The student wants to make 200 cm³ of 0.30 mol/dm³ sodium carbonate solution by diluting some of his original solution. What volume of his original solution will he need to use?

.... cm³

[3]

[Total 4 marks]

Exam Practice Tip

Questions involving concentrations of solutions are a whole lot easier if you're confident using the formulas for concentration in g/dm³ and in mol/dm³. That means not just remembering the formulas, but knowing how to rearrange them and how to convert between cm³ and dm³ and between moles and grams if you need to. If there are any of those skills you're not comfortable with, get practising — calculations can net you easy marks in the exams.

Chapter C5 — Chemical Analysis

Titrations

Warm-Up

The diagrams below show a titration experiment being set up.
Label the diagrams using the labels on the right. One label has been done for you.

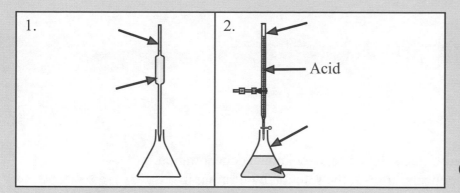

Solution containing an alkali and an indicator

Alkali   ~~Acid~~

Burette

Pipette

Conical flask

1 A student wants to find out the concentration of a solution of alkali by titrating it with an acid.

a) Identify which of the following statements is **false**. Place a tick (✓) in one box only.

Universal indicator is the most suitable indicator for use in titrations. ☐

Titrations can be used to determine the concentration of an unknown solution. ☐

Concentration can be measured in g/dm^3 or mol/dm^3. ☐

An indicator is usually used to identify the point of neutralisation in an acid-base titration. ☐

[1]

b) Explain why a burette is useful for identifying the end-point of a titration.

....

....

....

[2]

c) Here is the method the student uses for the titration:

> 1. Add the acid to the alkali from the burette a little at a time, regularly swirling the conical flask.
> 2. Record the volume of acid required to just make the indicator change colour.
> 3. Use this volume to calculate the concentration of the alkali.

Explain how the method should be changed to increase the accuracy of the results.

....

....

....

[2]

[Total 5 marks]

Chapter C5 — Chemical Analysis

2 A chemist completes a titration where 0.00850 mol of potassium hydroxide is neutralised by 0.0250 dm³ of sulfuric acid. The equation for the reaction is:

$$2KOH + H_2SO_4 \rightarrow K_2SO_4 + 2H_2O$$

Grade
6-7

What is the concentration of the sulfuric acid in g/dm³?
Place a tick (✓) in the box next to the correct answer.
Relative formula mass (M_r): $H_2SO_4 = 98.1$

0.170 g/dm³ ☐

16.7 g/dm³ ☐

1.66 g/dm³ ☐

17.3 g/dm³ ☐

[Total 1 mark]

3 Amy has a sodium hydroxide solution of an unknown concentration.
She plans to find the concentration of the solution by titrating it
with a 0.200 mol/dm³ standard solution of sulfuric acid.

Grade
7-9

a)* Describe how to carry out a titration, with reference to the equipment used.

....

....

....

....

....

....

....

....

....

....

....

[6]

b) It took 22.5 cm³ of the standard solution to neutralise 25.0 cm³ of sodium hydroxide solution.
Calculate the concentration of the sodium hydroxide. Give your answer to 3 significant figures.
The equation for the reaction is: $2NaOH + H_2SO_4 \rightarrow Na_2SO_4 + 2H_2O$

Concentration = ... mol/dm³
[3]

[Total 9 marks]

4 A student had a solution of sodium carbonate, Na_2CO_3, of unknown concentration. The student also had hydrochloric acid, HCl, with a concentration of 1.00 mol/dm³.
The equation for the reaction between sodium carbonate and hydrochloric acid is:

$$Na_2CO_3 + 2HCl \rightarrow 2NaCl + H_2O + CO_2$$

a) The student carried out an experiment to find out how much hydrochloric acid was needed to neutralise 25.0 cm³ of the sodium carbonate solution. They did the experiment 5 times.

Give **two** reasons why it is a good idea to repeat titrations several times.

....

....

....
[2]

b) The student's results are shown in the table below.
Calculate the mean volume of hydrochloric acid that was needed.
Ignore any anomalous results (ones that are not within 0.10 cm³ of each other.)

	Experiment Number				
	1	2	3	4	5
Volume of 1.00 mol/dm³ HCl (cm³)	12.95	12.50	12.25	12.55	12.45

Mean volume = ... cm³
[2]

c) Using your answer to part b), find the concentration of the sodium carbonate solution, in mol/dm³.

Concentration of sodium carbonate = ... mol/dm³
[6]
[Total 10 marks]

Exam Practice Tip

When you're working out the mean from a set of results, you should ignore any anomalous results. So if you get a question in your exam asking you to work out a mean, make sure you check for anomalous results before you start plugging numbers into your calculator. The question might help you out by reminding you to ignore anomalous results, but it might not, so make sure you're on the ball with it — don't get caught out.

Acids, Alkalis and pH

Warm-Up

Use the words below to fill in the gaps for the following paragraph on techniques to measure pH.

red

neutral

green   purple

more   less

Universal indicator will turn .... in strongly acidic solutions and .... in strongly alkaline solutions. In a .... solution, universal indicator will be green. A pH probe attached to a pH meter is .... accurate than universal indicator as it displays a numerical value for pH.

1   Indicators are substances that can be used to test the pH of a solution.   (Grade 4-6)

a) State the range of the pH scale.

....

[1]

b) What is an indicator?

....

....

[2]

[Total 3 marks]

2   Place a tick (✓) in the box next to the statement that is **false**.   (Grade 6-7)

Before using a pH probe, you should calibrate it by setting it to measure pH 7 in a sample of pure water.   ☐

pH probes give a numerical value for the pH of a solution.   ☐

You should wash a pH probe with a weak acid in between readings.   ☐

pH probes measure pH electronically.   ☐

[Total 1 mark]

3   Eleanor has a solution where the H^+ concentration is 0.0014 mol/dm³.   (Grade 7-9)

a) Place a tick (✓) in the box next to the value that will be closest to the pH of Eleanor's solution.

2 ☐   3 ☐   4 ☐   5 ☐

[1]

b) Eleanor measures the exact value of the pH of her solution. She then dilutes the solution until the concentration of H^+ ions is 0.00014 mol/dm³. Explain how she could tell by measuring the pH of her diluted solution that it has the desired concentration of H^+ ions.

....

[1]

[Total 2 marks]

Strong and Weak Acids

1 Methanoic acid, HCOOH, is a **weak acid**. (Grade 6-7)

a) Write a chemical equation to show how methanoic acid acts as a weak acid.

....

[2]

b) Predict whether the reaction of a piece of zinc with acid will take place faster with methanoic acid, or with a strong acid of the same concentration. Explain your answer.

....

....

....

....

....

[2]

[Total 4 marks]

2 Tamal has two beakers, each containing a sample of a different acid.
The acid in beaker X is **stronger** than the acid in beaker Y.
The acid in beaker Y is **more concentrated** than the acid in beaker X. (Grade 6-7)

Which of the following options could describe the contents of the two beakers?
Place a tick (✓) in the correct row.

Beaker X	Beaker Y	✓
0.002 mol/dm³ HCl	4.0 mol/dm³ CH₃COOH	
4.0 mol/dm³ HCl	0.002 mol/dm³ CH₃COOH	
0.002 mol/dm³ CH₃COOH	4.0 mol/dm³ HCl	
4.0 mol/dm³ CH₃COOH	0.002 mol/dm³ HCl	

[Total 1 mark]

3 Jackie is carrying out an experiment to measure how the pH of a strong acid is affected by its concentration. (Grade 7-9)

a) Jackie takes a sample of an acidic solution, **A**, made by dissolving a solid acid in deionised water. Which of the following could Jackie do to make his sample more concentrated?
Place a tick (✓) in the box next to the correct answer.

Add a more dilute solution of the acid to the sample. ☐

Add more water to the sample. ☐

Add more solution the same as A to the sample. ☐

Dissolve more solid acid in the sample. ☐

[Total 1 mark]

Chapter C6 — Making Useful Chemicals

Reactions of Acids

1 June reacts a soluble metal hydroxide and an acid together in a flask. *Grade 4-6*

a) Which of the following describes the products of this reaction?
Place a tick (✓) in the box next to the correct answer.

A salt and water. ☐

A salt and carbon dioxide gas. ☐

A salt, water and carbon dioxide gas. ☐

A salt and hydrogen gas. ☐

[1]

b) Name the type of reaction that takes place when an acid is mixed with an alkali.

....

[1]

[Total 2 marks]

2 Complete the table to show the chemical formulas of the salts created in the reactions involving the following acids. *Grade 6-7*

	Hydrochloric acid (HCl)	Nitric acid (HNO$_3$)	Sulfuric acid (H$_2$SO$_4$)
Zinc metal (Zn)	ZnCl$_2$	....	ZnSO$_4$
Calcium carbonate (CaCO$_3$)	CaCl$_2$	Ca(NO$_3$)$_2$	....
Sodium hydroxide (NaOH)	NaCl	NaNO$_3$	....
Potassium carbonate (K$_2$CO$_3$)	....	KNO$_3$	K$_2$SO$_4$

[Total 4 marks]

3 Pauline mixes zinc carbonate, ZnCO$_3$, with hydrochloric acid, HCl, and notes that the mixture starts to bubble as a gas is given off. *Grade 6-7*

a) What is the name of the gas that is responsible for the bubbles in the reaction?

....

[1]

b) Write a balanced chemical equation for the reaction between hydrochloric acid and zinc carbonate.

....

[2]

c) What is the name of the salt produced by the reaction?

....

[1]

[Total 4 marks]

Chapter C6 — Making Useful Chemicals

Making Salts

Warm-Up

Circle the **two** processes which would **not** be used to prepare
a pure, dry sample of a soluble salt from a solution of that salt.

titration

distillation

evaporation

filtration

1   Insoluble salts can be made by precipitation reactions.
Place a tick (✓) in the box next to the equation that describes a precipitation reaction.

Grade
4-6

$CuO_{(s)} + 2HCl_{(aq)} \rightarrow CuCl_{2\,(aq)} + H_2O_{(l)}$ ☐

$HCl_{(aq)} + NaOH_{(aq)} \rightarrow NaCl_{(aq)} + H_2O_{(l)}$ ☐

$2HNO_{3\,(aq)} + ZnCO_{3\,(s)} \rightarrow Zn(NO_3)_{2\,(aq)} + H_2O_{(l)} + CO_{2\,(g)}$ ☐

$Pb(NO_3)_{2\,(aq)} + 2NaCl_{(aq)} \rightarrow PbCl_{2\,(s)} + 2NaNO_{3\,(aq)}$ ☐

[Total 1 mark]

2   Jeremy is making a sample of silver chloride,
an insoluble salt, using an acid and a salt solution.

Grade
6-7

a)   Suggest an acid that Jeremy could use to make silver chloride.

....

[1]

b)   Once Jeremy has made the salt, he pours the whole
solid and salt solution into a filter funnel, as shown below.

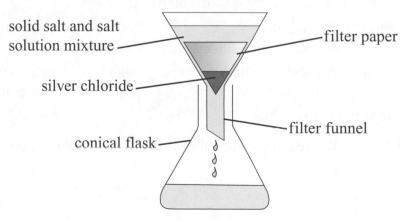

solid salt and salt
solution mixture

filter paper

silver chloride

filter funnel

conical flask

What has Jeremy done wrong? Explain how this will affect
the mass of solid salt that he collects from the solution.

....

....

....

[2]

[Total 3 marks]

Chapter C6 — Making Useful Chemicals

3 Davina reacts aqueous iron(III) nitrate solution, $Fe(NO_3)_3$, with aqueous sodium hydroxide solution, NaOH, to make an insoluble salt containing iron.

Grade 6-7

a) Write down the chemical formula of the insoluble salt.

....

[1]

b) Davina used the following method to prepare the salt:

> 1. Mix the sodium hydroxide solution with the iron(III) nitrate solution in a beaker and stir.
> 2. Line a filter funnel with filter paper and place it in a conical flask.
>   Pour the contents of the beaker into the filter paper.
> 3. Rinse the beaker with deionised water and tip this into the filter paper.
> 4. Rinse the contents of the filter paper with deionised water.

i) Explain why Davina rinsed the beaker and added the rinsings to the filter paper.

....

[1]

ii) After completing step 4, Davina wants to dry the solid product. Suggest how she could do this.

....

[1]

[Total 3 marks]

4 The following steps describe how you would produce a pure, dry sample of magnesium sulfate, $MgSO_4$, from solid magnesium hydroxide and dilute sulfuric acid.

Grade 6-7

The steps of the procedure are not in the correct order.

1 Slowly heat the solution to evaporate off some of the water.

2 Filter the solid off and dry it.

3 Filter out the excess solid using a filter funnel and filter paper.

4 Add magnesium hydroxide to a flask containing sulfuric acid until no more of the metal hydroxide reacts (at this point, the excess solid will just sink to the bottom of the flask).

5 Leave the solution to crystallise.

a) Put the steps in the correct order, by writing the numbers 1-5 in the boxes below.

[2]

b) Write a balanced symbol equation, including state symbols, that describes the reaction between magnesium hydroxide, $Mg(OH)_2$, and dilute sulfuric acid, H_2SO_4.

....

[3]

[Total 5 marks]

5 Andy is making a sample of sodium nitrate, NaNO₃, by reacting together sodium carbonate, Na₂CO₃, and dilute nitric acid, HNO₃. *Grade 6-7*

a) Sodium nitrate is a soluble salt. Explain what is meant by the term 'soluble' in this context.

....

[1]

b) Write a balanced chemical equation for this reaction.

....

[2]

c) Andy uses a titration method to add a sodium carbonate solution to the acid until he reaches the end-point, which is shown by a change in colour of an indicator in the solution. He then crystallises the solution to obtain the salt. Will this produce a pure sample of the salt? Explain your answer.

....

....

[1]

[Total 4 marks]

6 Copper sulfate is a soluble salt that can be made by the reaction between dilute sulfuric acid, H₂SO₄, and copper oxide, CuO. *Grade 7-9*

a) Write a balanced chemical equation for the reaction between dilute sulfuric acid and copper oxide.

....

[2]

b)* Outline how you could prepare a pure, dry sample of copper sulfate in the lab from dilute sulfuric acid and copper oxide.

....

....

....

....

....

....

....

....

....

....

[6]

[Total 8 marks]

Exam Practice Tip

There are lots of methods to make salts, depending on whether the products or reactants are soluble or insoluble. Using the wrong one will get you in a right pickle, so make sure you know when to use each method.

Chapter C6 — Making Useful Chemicals

Rates of Reactions

1 This question is about the rate of a chemical reaction between two reactants, one of which is in solution, and one of which is a solid.

a) Which of the following changes would **not** cause the rate of the chemical reaction to increase? Place a tick (✓) in the box next to the correct answer.

Decreasing the concentration of the solution. ☐

Heating the reaction mixture to a higher temperature. ☐

Adding a catalyst. ☐

Grinding the solid reactant so that it forms a fine powder. ☐

[1]

b) What is the name given to the minimum amount of energy which particles must have if they are to react when they collide?

....

[1]

[Total 2 marks]

2 The graph below shows how the mass of gas lost from a reaction vessel changes over time, for the same reaction under different conditions.

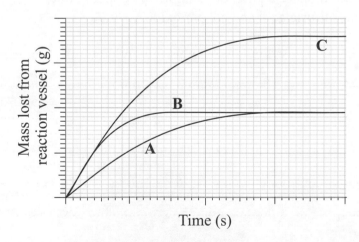

Time (s)

a) State which of the reactions, **A**, **B** or **C**:

i) Produced the most product: ....

ii) Finished first: ....

iii) Started at the slowest rate: ....

[3]

b) On the graph, sketch the curve you would expect to see if reaction C was repeated at a higher temperature, but with all the other conditions unchanged.

[3]

[Total 6 marks]

Chapter C6 — Making Useful Chemicals

3   Enzymes are biological catalysts.   **Grade 6-7**

a) Give **one** limitation of using enzymes as industrial catalysts.

....

....

                                                                [1]

b) The reaction profile for a reaction with and without a catalyst is shown below.
Identify what each of the labels, A–D, show.

A: ....

B: ....

C: ....

D: ....

                                                                [4]

c) The graph below shows the rate of a reaction in the presence of an enzyme at different temperatures.

At what temperature is the rate of the reaction fastest?

....

                                                                [1]

                                                   [Total 6 marks]

4   Explain, using collision theory, what effect each of the following changes would have on the rate of a reaction between gases in a closed system: **Grade 7-9**

a) Increasing the volume of the reaction vessel.

....

....

....

                                                                 [3]

b) Increasing the temperature at which the reaction is carried out.

....

....

....

                                                                 [3]

                                                   [Total 6 marks]

Reaction Rate Experiments

1   Lukas wants to investigate how the rate of a particular reaction is affected
    by temperature. The reaction produces a precipitate, so he plans to time
    how long it takes for the solution to go cloudy at each temperature.

    Grade 4-6

   a) What is the dependent variable in this experiment?

   ....
   [1]

   b) What is the independent variable in this experiment?

   ....
   [1]

   c) Suggest **one** variable that would have to be controlled in this experiment to make it a fair test.

   ....
   [1]

   d) The reaction also produces a gas. State whether it would be more accurate to measure the rate
       of the reaction by timing how long it takes for the solution to go cloudy, or by timing how long it
       takes a volume of gas to be produced. Explain your answer.

   ....

   ....
   [2]
   [Total 5 marks]

2   Laiza is investigating the rate of a reaction between two solutions that produces a gas.

    Grade 6-7

   a) She measures out volumes of both reactants and gently heats each solution separately in a water
       bath to 50 °C. Outline a method that Laiza could follow to monitor the rate of the reaction.

   ....

   ....

   ....
   [3]

   b) During the reaction, 10.60 cm^3 of gas is produced in 40.0 s.
       Calculate the mean rate of reaction during this time. Include units in your answer.

   rate = ... units = ...
   [3]
   [Total 6 marks]

Chapter C6 — Making Useful Chemicals

3 The rate of a reaction between two solutions was investigated by monitoring the amount of one of the reactants, A, at regular intervals. A graph of the results is shown below.

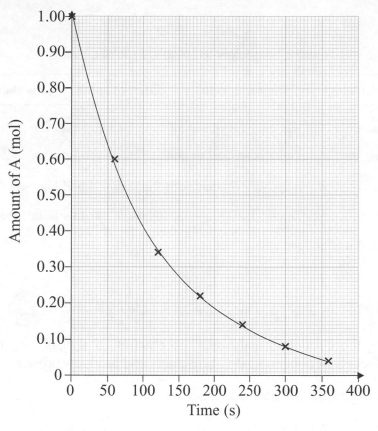

a) Use the graph to calculate the rate of the reaction at exactly 50 s after the start of the reaction. Give this rate to two significant figures. Include units in your answer.

rate = ... units = ...

[4]

b) In the same way calculate the rate of the reaction at exactly 200 s after the start of the reaction.

rate = ... units = ...

[4]

c) Reactant A is coloured so the amount of reactant A in the mixture can be calculated from the amount of light passing through the solution. Name a piece of equipment that could be used to monitor how the amount of reactant A changes during the reaction.

....

[1]

[Total 9 marks]

Chapter C6 — Making Useful Chemicals

Dynamic Equilibrium

Warm-Up

Choose from the words in the box below to complete the paragraph.

| increases | change | the same rate | different rates | decreases | not change |

In a reversible reaction, as the concentrations of the reactants fall, the rate of the forward

reaction .... and as the concentrations of the products rise, the rate of the

backward reaction .... When both the forward and backward reactions are

going at ...., they are at equilibrium. At this point, the concentrations

of the reactants and products will ....

1   Dynamic equilibrium can only be achieved in reversible reactions.   (Grade 4-6)

    a) Compare the rates of the forwards and backwards reactions at dynamic equilibrium.
       State how this affects the concentrations of reactants and products present at dynamic equilibrium.

....

....

[2]

    b) Dynamic equilibrium can only be reached in a closed system.
       Explain what is meant by a 'closed system'.

....

....

[1]

[Total 3 marks]

2   An aqueous solution of blue copper(II) ions can react with chloride ions to form a yellow   (Grade 6-7)
    copper compound. The ionic equation for this reaction is: $Cu^{2+} + 4Cl^- \rightleftharpoons [CuCl_4]^{2-}$

    a) What does the symbol '$\rightleftharpoons$' mean in this reaction?

....

[1]

    b) A solution containing copper(II) ions is mixed with a solution containing chloride ions in a flask.
       The solution quickly turns green. When observed for a few minutes no further change in colour
       can be seen. Explain these observations.

....

....

....

[2]

[Total 3 marks]

Changing the Position of Equilibrium

Predict whether the changes below would result in there being more reactants or more products at equilibrium for the reaction: $N_{2(g)} + 3H_{2(g)} \rightleftharpoons 2NH_{3(g)}$. The forward reaction is exothermic.

Increasing the temperature: ....

Decreasing the pressure: ....

Increasing the concentration of N_2: ....

1   The position of equilibrium of a reaction is dependent on the conditions used to carry out the reaction.

Grade 4-6

a)   State the general rule about the effect of changing the conditions of a reversible reaction at equilibrium.

....

[1]

b)   State **two** conditions you could change in order to alter the position of equilibrium of a reaction that happens in solution.

....

....

[2]

[Total 3 marks]

2   A mixture of iodine monochloride (ICl) and chlorine is sealed in a gas syringe. The gases react in a reversible reaction to form iodine trichloride (ICl_3) and eventually reach an equilibrium. The equation for the reaction is: $ICl_{(l)} + Cl_{2(g)} \rightleftharpoons ICl_{3(s)}$.

Grade 6-7

a)   Given that the forward reaction is exothermic, explain how the relative quantities of ICl and ICl_3 would change if the mixture was heated, and all other conditions remained the same.

....

....

....

[2]

b)   Explain how the relative quantities of ICl and ICl_3 would change if the plunger were pushed into the syringe, and the temperature remained constant.

....

....

....

[3]

[Total 5 marks]

Chapter C6 — Making Useful Chemicals

3 Dinitrogen tetroxide (N_2O_4) is a colourless gas. It decomposes in a reversible reaction to form the brown gas, nitrogen dioxide (NO_2). The reaction equation is: $N_2O_{4(g)} \rightleftharpoons 2NO_{2(g)}$.

Grade 7-9

a) When a sample of N_2O_4 is left to decompose in a sealed tube, a pale brown colour can be seen. If this mixture is heated, the colour becomes a darker brown. Explain this observation and predict whether the forward reaction is exothermic or endothermic.

....

....

....

[3]

b) Explain how you would expect the colour of the equilibrium mixture to change if the pressure of the mixture is decreased, and all other conditions are kept the same.

....

....

....

[3]

[Total 6 marks]

4 Yellow iron(III) ions and colourless thiocyanate ions react reversibly in solution to form dark red iron thiocyanate: $Fe^{3+}_{(aq)} + SCN^-_{(aq)} \rightleftharpoons FeSCN^{2+}_{(aq)}$

Grade 7-9

The following observations are made about this reaction:
1. When a yellow solution containing Fe^{3+} ions and a colourless solution containing SCN^- ions are mixed, a pale red colour forms which initially grows darker but then stays constant.
2. When more Fe^{3+} ions are added to the solution it initially becomes more orangey in colour but then grows darker red than before the Fe^{3+} was added and remains like this.
3. If $FeSCN^{2+}$ ions are added to the solution it initially becomes darker in colour but then becomes more orangey.

Explain what is happening in each of these observations.

Observation 1: ....

....

Observation 2: ....

....

Observation 3: ....

....

[Total 6 marks]

Exam Practice Tip

Working out what happens to the position of an equilibrium when you change the conditions can be a bit of a brain twister. Just remember that for any change that's made, the reaction will try to do the opposite. So if you increase the temperature, more of the endothermic reaction will happen, if you increase the pressure, the equilibrium will move to the side where there are fewer moles of gas, and if you increase the concentration of a reactant, you'll get more products.

Chapter C6 — Making Useful Chemicals

Atom Economy

1 Magnesium chloride has a variety of applications. It can be produced by several different reactions. Three reactions are shown below.

$$X \qquad Mg + 2HCl \rightarrow MgCl_2 + H_2$$
$$Y \qquad MgCO_3 + 2HCl \rightarrow MgCl_2 + H_2O + CO_2$$
$$Z \qquad MgO + 2HCl \rightarrow MgCl_2 + H_2O$$

(Relative atomic masses: Mg = 24, Cl = 35.5, O = 16, C = 12, H = 1)

a) i) Calculate the relative formula mass of magnesium chloride.

relative formula mass = ...

[1]

ii) Calculate the atom economy reaction X. Give your answer to 2 significant figures.

Atom economy = ... %

[3]

iii) Calculate the atom economy reaction Y. Give your answer to 2 significant figures.

Atom economy = ... %

[3]

iv) Calculate the atom economy reaction Z. Give your answer to 2 significant figures.

Atom economy = ... %

[3]

b) i) A scientist from the company says, "We should choose the process which has the highest atom economy". Suggest why the company might prefer a high atom economy.

....

....

....

....

....

[4]

ii) Suggest **two** other factors that the company might consider when choosing a process to use.

....

[2]

[Total 16 marks]

Chapter C6 — Making Useful Chemicals

Industrial Processes

1 An industrial company is researching the implications of using crude oil as a starting material. Grade **4-6**

a) Give **one** disadvantage of using crude oil as a source of raw materials.

....

[1]

b) A company discovers it can synthesise a crude oil substitute using a reaction that occurs at high temperatures and pressures. Suggest why using the crude oil substitute as a starting material may not be economically viable.

....

....

[1]

[Total 2 marks]

2 The graph below shows the effect of pH and temperature on the rate of a reaction carried out by an industrial company. Grade **7-9**

Rate

pH

Temperature

| pH | 0 | 2 | 4 | 6 | 8 | 10 | 12 |
| Temp (°C) | 0 | 10 | 20 | 30 | 40 | 50 | 60 |

a) From the conditions shown on the graph, what is the optimum pH and temperature for the reaction to maximise the rate?

pH = ...   Temperature = ...

[2]

b) The yield of this reaction is at its highest when the temperature is 10 °C.
Explain whether or not it is sensible to carry the reaction out at this temperature.

....

....

[1]

c) Another of the company's processes involves a reaction between two gases.
The company decides to increase the pressure that they carry this reaction out at.
Give **one** advantage and **one** disadvantage of increasing the pressure.

....

....

....

[2]

[Total 5 marks]

Sustainability

1 Aluminium is a metal which is obtained from the raw material bauxite. Bauxite needs to be extracted from below the ground. *Grade 4-6*

a) Recycling aluminium is more **sustainable** than producing new aluminium. What does this mean?

....

....

[1]

b) Suggest **two** reasons why the mining of bauxite may not be a sustainable process.

....

....

[2]

[Total 3 marks]

2 Ethanol is a type of alcohol which can be made in different ways. One method is the hydration of ethene using steam and another is the fermentation of glucose. *Grade 6-7*

Details of both reactions are shown in the table below.

	Hydration of Ethene	Fermentation of Glucose
Reaction equation	$C_2H_4 + H_2O \rightleftharpoons CH_3CH_2OH$	$C_6H_{12}O_6 \rightarrow 2CH_3CH_2OH + 2CO_2$
Raw material	crude oil	plant material, e.g. sugar cane
Reaction conditions	300 °C, 60-70 atmospheres	30-40 °C, atmospheric pressure

a) Using the information given above, compare the sustainability of the two processes.

....

....

....

....

....

....

....

....

[6]

b) Industrial hydration of ethene is a continuous process in which the reactants are passed through a reactor. As it passes through the reactor, only 5% of the ethene is converted to ethanol. Suggest what can be done to improve the sustainability of the reaction.

....

[1]

[Total 7 marks]

Chapter C6 — Making Useful Chemicals

The Haber Process

1 The Haber process is an important chemical process. (Grade 4-6)

a) What is the product of the Haber process?

....

[1]

b) One of the substances used as a reactant in the Haber process is nitrogen.
Place a tick (✓) in the box next to the raw material from which nitrogen is obtained.

coal ☐   rocks ☐   crude oil ☐   seawater ☐   air ☐

[1]

[Total 2 marks]

2 The Haber process is carried out at a pressure of 200 atm and a temperature of 450 °C. (Grade 7-9)

a) i) A company increases the temperature in the reaction vessel for the Haber process to 580 °C.
Place a tick (✓) in the box next to the result of this change in temperature.

Higher rate of reaction. ☐   No change in the rate of reaction. ☐

Lower rate of reaction. ☐   Impossible to predict. ☐

[1]

ii) The company thinks the increase in temperature will increase the yield of product from the
Haber process. Do you agree or disagree with the company? Explain your answer.

....

....

....

[2]

b) In a bid to make the process cheaper, the company decides to
reduce the pressure at which they carry out the Haber process.

Give **two** disadvantages of using a low pressure to carry out the Haber process.

....

....

[2]

c) The Haber process uses an iron catalyst. How does the iron catalyst affect:

i) the rate?...

[1]

ii) the yield?...

[1]

[Total 7 marks]

Chapter C6 — Making Useful Chemicals

Fertilisers

Place a tick (✓) in the box to show whether each of the following statements about synthetic fertilisers is true or false.

Statement	True	False
Synthetic fertilisers are made by reacting an acid with a metal.		
Synthetic fertilisers contain salts.		
The three main essential elements in synthetic fertilisers are nitrogen, phosphorus and sodium.		
Many synthetic fertilisers are made using ammonia.		

1 Fertilisers can be produced both in the laboratory and on an industrial scale.

Grade 6-7

a) Which of the following statements about the production of fertilisers is **false**?
Place a tick (✓) in the box next to the false statement.

Laboratory processes produce fertilisers in batches. ☐

The industrial production of fertilisers uses a titration method using burettes. ☐

Industrial production of fertilisers is usually continuous. ☐

Laboratory production produces smaller quantities of fertilisers compared to industrial production. ☐

[1]

b) Give **one** advantage of making fertilisers using by-products from other processes as the reactants.

....

[1]

c) To meet the large demand, the processes used during the production of fertilisers in industry differ from those used in the lab. However, both types of production include similar stages. State **three** steps in fertiliser production which are shared by both lab and industrial processes.

....

....

[3]

d) Fertiliser factories often use 'integrated processes' to make fertilisers. What does this term mean?

....

....

[2]

[Total 7 marks]

Chapter C6 — Making Useful Chemicals

114

2 Derek has just bought a vegetable farm. The farm is located next to a river which runs alongside another farm owned by farmer Owen.

a) Derek decides to use a synthetic fertiliser to help replace essential elements lost from the soil. Give **one** way that the elements may have been lost and explain why they need replacing.

....

....

[2]

b) Derek had considered using manure to fertilise his crops before he opted for the synthetic variety. Give **two** disadvantages associated with the use of natural fertilisers.

....

....

[2]

c) Farmer Owen advises Derek to not fertilise his fields when heavy rainfall is forecast in the following 48 hours since fertiliser can get washed away before it is fully absorbed by the soil. Explain the possible environmental impacts if Derek ignores this advice.

....

....

....

....

....

....

....

[5]

[Total 9 marks]

3 Fertilisers contain salts, many of which are produced using ammonia.

a) The Haber process is used to produce ammonia. Suggest why it is said that without the Haber process, it would be impossible to grow enough food to feed the population of the world.

....

....

....

[3]

b) Place a tick (✓) in the box next to the salt that would **not** be useful as a fertiliser. Explain your answer.

☐ $Ca(NO_3)_2$ ☐ CuI ☐ KNO_3 ☐ $(NH_4)_3PO_4$

....

....

[2]

[Total 5 marks]

Mixed Questions

1   The displayed formula of an organic compound is shown below.

$$H-\underset{\underset{H}{|}}{\overset{\overset{H}{|}}{C}}-\underset{\underset{H}{|}}{\overset{\overset{H}{|}}{C}}-\underset{\underset{H}{|}}{\overset{\overset{H}{|}}{C}}-C\overset{\displaystyle \nearrow O}{\underset{\displaystyle \searrow O-H}{}}$$

a)   Which homologous series does this compound belong to?

....
                                                                                                        [1]

b)   Find the relative formula mass of this compound.
     (relative atomic masses: C = 12.0, H = 1.0, O = 16.0)

relative formula mass = ...
                                                                                                        [1]

c)   What is the empirical formula of this compound?

....
                                                                                                        [2]
                                                                                        [Total 4 marks]

2   Bromine is a Group 7 element that exists as molecules of Br_2.   Grade 4-6

a)   Complete the diagram below to give a dot and cross diagram that shows the bonding in Br_2.
     You only need to show the outer electron shells.

Br   Br

                                                                                                        [2]

b)   Which of the following describes the structure of bromine?
     Place a tick (✓) in the box next to the correct answer.

giant ionic ☐   giant covalent ☐   simple molecular ☐   fullerene ☐
lattice   structure   substance
                                                                                                        [1]

c)   What is the state of bromine at room temperature and pressure?

....
                                                                                                        [1]
                                                                                        [Total 4 marks]

3 Sulfur dioxide, SO$_2$, is formed by the combustion of sulfur. (Grade 4-6)

   a) i) Name **one** source of sulfur dioxide air pollution.

   ....

   ....

   [1]

   ii) Give **one** way in which sulfur dioxide pollution can create a hazard to the environment.

   ....

   ....

   [1]

   b) Sulfur dioxide reacts with oxygen gas in a reversible reaction to form sulfur trioxide, SO$_3$.
      Write a balanced symbol equation for this reaction.

   ....

   [2]

   [Total 4 marks]

4 The table below shows the properties of some polymers. (Grade 6-7)

Polymer	Type of monomer(s)	Response when heated	Hardness
A	alkene	softens	flexible
B	alkene	does not soften	rigid
C	dicarboxylic acid and diol	softens	rigid

   a) Explain what the difference in the response to heating tells you about the bonding in **A** and **B**.

   ....

   ....

   [2]

   b) Outline the formation of polymer **A** and polymer **C** from their monomers.

   ....

   ....

   ....

   ....

   ....

   [3]

   c) Explain which polymer would be most suitable for making a plastic mug for hot drinks.

   ....

   ....

   ....

   [3]

   [Total 8 marks]

Mixed Questions

5 Pentane, C_5H_{12}, and decane, $C_{10}H_{22}$, are both hydrocarbons in the same homologous series.

Grade 6-7

a) Which homologous series do pentane and decane belong to?

....
[1]

b) Name a process that could be used to produce pentane from decane.

....
[1]

c) Predict, with reasoning, whether pentane or decane will have a **higher** boiling point.

....

....

....
[2]

d) Write a balanced symbol equation for the complete combustion
of pentane in oxygen to form carbon dioxide and water.

....
[2]

[Total 6 marks]

6 Rubidium is an element from Group 1 of the periodic table.
Fluorine is an element from Group 7.
Rubidium metal, Rb, and fluorine gas, F_2, react violently to produce a single product.

Grade 6-7

a) Write a balanced symbol equation for the reaction of rubidium metal with fluorine gas.
Include state symbols in your answer.

....
[3]

b) Name the type of bonding present in the product of this reaction.

....
[1]

c) The reaction between rubidium and fluorine is extremely 'exothermic'.
Describe what this term means, in terms of the energy levels of the products and reactants.

....

....
[1]

d) Fluorine is in Period 2 of the periodic table. Give the electronic structure of fluorine.

....
[1]

[Total 6 marks]

PRACTICAL

7 When the following reaction is carried out in an unsealed reaction flask, the mass of the contents of the flask changes over the course of the reaction:

$$2Al_{(s)} + 3H_2SO_{4(aq)} \rightarrow Al_2(SO_4)_{3(aq)} + 3H_{2(g)}$$

a) Write the ionic equation for the reaction.

....

[2]

b) Hydrogen is produced in the reaction. Describe the test you would use to identify hydrogen gas.

....

....

....

[2]

c) The volume of gas produced by the reaction mixture can be used to investigate how the concentration of acid affects the rate of the reaction. Write a method that the student could use to carry out this experiment.

....

....

....

....

....

....

[6]

d) At the start of an experiment, the gas syringe was empty. After 30 s, it contained 12.0 cm³ of gas. Calculate the mean rate of reaction during this time.

Mean rate = ... cm³/s

[2]

e) A scientist wants to produce a batch of aluminium sulfate by reacting aluminium with an excess of sulfuric acid. A chemical supplier offers three options to provide the quantity of aluminium she needs. Place a tick (✓) in the box to show the option that will allow the scientist to complete her reaction in the **shortest** time.

1 aluminium cube with side length 8 cm. ☐

8 aluminium cubes, each with side length 4 cm. ☐

64 aluminium cubes, each with side length 2 cm. ☐

They will all take the same length of time. ☐

[1]

[Total 13 marks]

8 Some elements have several different isotopes. The bar chart below shows the percentage of the atoms of some elements that exist as each of their isotopes.

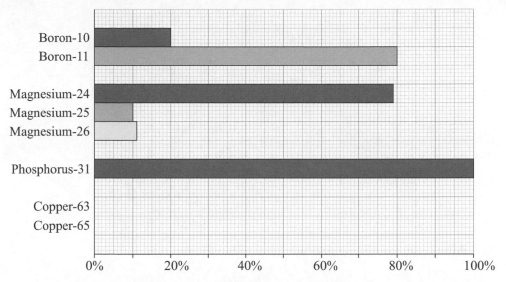

a) 69% of copper atoms are copper-63 and the rest are copper-65.
Complete the bar chart above by adding bars for the two isotopes of copper.

[2]

b) Explain why the relative atomic mass of phosphorus is a whole number, while the relative atomic masses of boron, magnesium and copper are not.

....

....

....

....

....

....

[3]

c) Use the bar chart to calculate the relative atomic mass of magnesium.
Give your answer to three significant figures.

relative atomic mass = ...

[3]

d) The atomic number of copper is 29. Copper can form ions with a 2+ charge.
How many electrons are there in one Cu^{2+} ion? Explain your answer.

....

....

....

[2]

[Total 10 marks]

Mixed Questions

9   Zinc is a metal with applications including the corrosion prevention of iron and steel. Before it can be used, it needs to be extracted from its ore. The process flow chart below shows the steps involved in the extraction of zinc from zinc sulfide (ZnS).

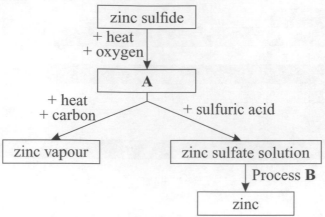

a) Name substance **A**.

   ....
   [1]

b) Give **one** pollutant that can be produced during the reduction of substance **A** with carbon.

   ....
   [1]

c) When zinc sulfide is roasted, sulfur dioxide is produced as a by-product. This can be further processed to form sulfuric acid. Suggest **one** way that the sustainability of the process would increase if this sulfuric acid was used to dissolve product **A** to form zinc sulfate solution.

   ....

   ....
   [1]

d) Suggest a technique that could be used to carry out the step marked 'Process **B**'.

   ....
   [1]

e) Give the chemical formula for zinc sulfate.

   ....
   [1]

f) i) Magnesium is another metal that needs to be extracted from its ore.
       Explain why magnesium cannot be extracted by heating its ore with carbon.

   ....
   [2]

   ii) Give the ionic equation for the reaction between magnesium and zinc sulfate solution. Include state symbols in your answer.

   ....
   [2]

   [Total 9 marks]

10 Andre wants to prepare a sample of silver chloride, AgCl, an insoluble salt.
To do this, he mixes solutions of barium chloride, $BaCl_2$, and silver nitrate, $AgNO_3$.

Grade 6-7

a) Complete the following equation for Andre's reaction by adding state symbols.

$$BaCl_2(..........) + 2AgNO_3(..........) \rightarrow 2AgCl(..........) + Ba(NO_3)_2 (..........)$$

[1]

b) When the reaction is complete, Andre wants to obtain a pure sample of silver chloride.

i) Andre suggests using crystallisation to separate silver chloride from the
reaction mixture. Explain why this would be an **unsuitable** method.

....

....

....

[2]

ii) Suggest a suitable method Andre could use to obtain a pure
sample of silver chloride from the reaction mixture.

....

[1]

c) Calculate the atom economy of Andre's reaction to make silver chloride.
Give your answer to three significant figures.
(relative atomic masses: Ag = 107.9, Cl = 35.5, Ba = 137.3, N = 14.0, O = 16.0)

atom economy = ...%

[4]

d) By using a suitable method to separate the mixture, Andre obtains 21.51 g of silver chloride.
Using the masses of reactants, Andre calculated that he should have produced
28.68 g of silver chloride. Calculate his percentage yield of silver chloride.

percentage yield = ...%

[2]

e) Andre decides to test the purity of his silver chloride. He wants to do this
by measuring the melting point of a number of 'representative samples'.
Describe what this term means and why it is important.

....

....

....

[2]

[Total 12 marks]

Mixed Questions

11 Iron(II) sulfate, $FeSO_4$, is a compound of the transition metal iron. (Grade 7-9) **PRACTICAL**

a) Describe a test you could carry out to confirm the identity of the cation. State any observations you would expect. Include the balanced ionic equation, with state symbols, for the reaction.

....

....

....

....

[5]

b) Describe a test you could carry out to confirm the identity of the anion. State any observations you would expect to make. Include the balanced ionic equation, with state symbols, for the reaction.

....

....

....

....

[6]

c) Name and describe the bonding present in the solid forms of pure iron and iron(II) sulfate.

....

....

....

....

....

[4]

d) Iron is used as a catalyst in the Haber process.

   i) Explain what a catalyst does.

....

....

....

[2]

   ii) Discuss why the use of a catalyst is important in the Haber process.

....

....

....

....

[3]

[Total 20 marks]

Mixed Questions

12 A hydrogen-oxygen fuel cell is a type of electrical cell.
Hydrogen-oxygen fuel cells produce energy from a redox reaction.

The equation for the reaction is:

$$2H_2 + O_2 \rightarrow 2H_2O$$

a) Place a tick (✓) in the box next to the statement which is **false**.

Hydrogen-oxygen fuel cells produce electricity more efficiently than power stations. ☐

Hydrogen-oxygen fuel cells do not directly produce any pollutants. ☐

Hydrogen-oxygen fuel cells use a turbine to generate electricity. ☐

Use of hydrogen as a fuel for cars may be limited because hydrogen gas is difficult to store. ☐

[1]

b) The table below shows the energies of the bonds involved in the reaction shown above.

Bond	Bond Energy (kJ/mol)
O=O	498
H–H	436
O–H	463

Calculate the energy change for the reaction which takes place in the hydrogen-oxygen fuel cell.

energy change = ... kJ/mol
[3]

c) A scientist recorded the amount of oxygen used by a fuel cell over a certain period of time.
The quantity of oxygen used occupied 156 dm³ at room temperature and pressure.
Calculate the mass of water produced if all of the oxygen reacted.

1 mole of gas has a volume of 24 dm³ at room temperature and pressure.
(relative atomic masses: H = 1.0, O = 16.0)

mass = ... g
[4]

[Total 8 marks]

Mixed Questions

13 Boron nitride, BN, is a compound which can form giant covalent structures. Two forms of boron nitride are shown below.

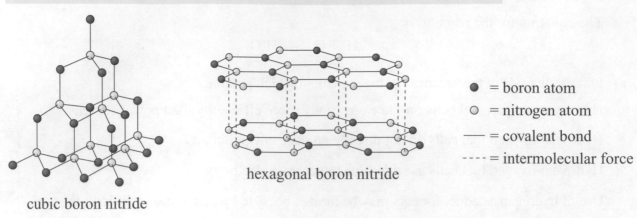

cubic boron nitride

hexagonal boron nitride

● = boron atom
○ = nitrogen atom
— = covalent bond
---- = intermolecular force

a) One of the two forms of boron nitride shown above is used to make drill bits. The other can be used as a lubricant. Using your knowledge of similar giant covalent structures to suggest which is which, complete the following sentences using either 'cubic' or 'hexagonal'.

i) .... boron nitride is used to make cutting tools.

ii) .... boron nitride is used as a lubricant.

[1]

b) Explain why the structure of boron nitride you have suggested in part a) i) would make it suitable to use to make drill bits.

....

....

....

....

[2]

c) Explain why the structure of boron nitride you have suggested in part a) ii) makes it suitable to use as a lubricant.

....

....

....

....

[2]

d) The main difference between the properties of hexagonal boron nitride and the closest equivalent carbon structure is that hexagonal boron nitride cannot conduct electricity, but its carbon equivalent can. What does this difference suggest about the structure of hexagonal boron nitride?

....

....

[1]

[Total 6 marks]

Mixed Questions